Enjoy This Title

The Nashua Public Library is free to all
cardholders. If you live, work, pay taxes,
or are a full-time student in Nashua you
qualify for a library card.

Increase the library's usefulness by returning
material on or before the 'date due.'

If you've enjoyed your experience with
the library and its many resources and
services, please tell others.

@ Nashua Public Library
2 Court Street, Nashua, NH 03060
603-589-4600, www.nashua.lib.nh.us

GAYLORD

womenomics

[*How to stop juggling and struggling and finally start living and working the way you really want*]

womenomics

Write Your
Own Rules for
Success

CLAIRE SHIPMAN *and*

KATTY KAY

HARPER
BUSINESS

An Imprint of HarperCollins*Publishers*

This book is designed for general information purposes only. All situations are different, and there is no such thing as "one size fits all" advice. The authors and the publisher assume no responsibility for any damages or losses incurred during or as a result of following the information contained herein.

FIRST EDITION

Designed by Janet M. Evans

Library of Congress Cataloging-in-Publication Data

Shipman, Claire
    Womenomics / Claire Shipman, Katty Kay.—1st ed.
        p. cm.
    . ISBN 978-0-06-169718-0
        1. Women—Employment. 2. Success in business. 3. Work and family. 4. Success. I. Kay, Katty. II. Title.
    HD6053.S534 2009
    650.1082—dc22   2008052484

09 10 11 12 13 OV/RRD   10 9 8 7 6 5 4 3 2 1

For Tom

And for F, M, J and P,

With so much love, Katty.

*For my father, Morgan, who taught me the thrill
of a life of the mind.*

*For my mother, Christie, who showed me the joy
of a life of the heart.*

*For my husband, Jay, who's encouraged, with
great humor and patience and love, my struggle
to pursue both.*

*And for Hugo and Della, who've managed to
shatter everything I thought I knew, and rearrange
it into a design that's suddenly, brilliantly clear.*

Love, Claire

ACKNOWLEDGMENTS

Womenomics would never have been possible without all of the women across America who shared their stories, trials, and triumphs with us. You were the fuel for the book, and we thank you all. We'd be on the phone for a quick interview, and find ourselves still talking hours later, as we uncovered common experiences and traded advice with strangers turned friends. The passion and instant bonding this subject can inspire came as a surprise even to us, and also made clear just how powerful the need is for a book like this.

So, Laura Bates, Linda Brooks (name changed to protect identity), Chandra Dhandapani, Miriam Decker (name changed to protect identity), Jennifer Dickey, Robin Ehlers, Stephanie Hampton, Christine Heenan, Anne Hurst, Melissa James, Jennifer Keisling, Angelique Krembs, Christy Runningen, Sarah Slusser, Maria Souder, Lauren Tyler, Julie Wellner, Barbara Williams, and Jennifer Winell—thank you. Your voices speak for women everywhere.

The project was not all estrogen driven, however. Our agent, Rafe Sagalyn, was invaluable to the birth and continued nurturing of *Womenomics*. As much as any of our women, he instantly "got" our concept, and became a passionate advocate. Rafe, you've been an indispensable guide through the publishing-world maze, a brilliant brainstorming partner, and a friend with a generous sense of humor.

Rafe also introduced us to our editor at HarperCollins, Hollis Heimbouch. From the moment we first sat down with her, we knew Hollis was the woman for *Womenomics*. She's everything we'd been warned editors are not anymore: hands-on, readily available, and full of savvy editorial guidance. Thank you for your vision.

The entire team at HarperCollins was simply brilliant and so supportive. Ben Steinberg, Matt Inman, Angie Lee, Paul Olsewski, Leslie Cohen, Shawn Nicholls, Doug Jones, Richard Ljoenes, Steve Ross, and Margot Schupf—how lucky we are that you took on *Womenomics* not as a job, but as a cause.

Naturally, we'd hardly be practicing Womenomics if we didn't delegate some of the work on this book. Many, many thanks to Lizette Baghdadi, Ashley Rindsburg, Erin Delmore, Jessica Nell Hayes, Chloe Abshire, and Jocelyn Phillips whose diligent and resourceful help with research and editing and transcribing literally got us to deadline.

We'd also like to thank Valerie Jarrett, Geraldine Laybourne, and Meg Whitman, who graciously gave us their time and take on the view from the top as well as the middle. And of course Michelle Obama, who has been such an open advocate for change, and who now, we hope, will be able to give this issue the attention it deserves.

And major thanks to both the BBC and ABC, who've offered us incredible opportunities and the chance for some balance in our lives. Not to mention the flexibility and latitude we needed to put *Womenomics* on paper.

Katty: I would like to thank my mother, Shirley Kay, who repeatedly defied cultural norms and establishment protocol to carve out a career as a journalist in the Arab world, one of the toughest places for women to work, while doggedly making time to raise four children. And my sister, Gigi Kay, who mixes ferocious professional drive with an innate determination to measure her career by her own standards, no one else's.

I am very proud of them both and immensely lucky to have their paths to follow in. My family in Washington was patient and understanding during a long, busy year. They put up with the travel of an election campaign followed by the deadlines for this book. And it would not have been possible without Awa M'Bow who looked after them all in my absence. Thank you, all of you.

Claire: Even as she raises her own child, and makes award-winning films, my sister, Susannah, is often forced to play the role of parent in our two-sibling family. And she did so brilliantly last year, cheering me on through an exhilarating and difficult twelve months. And Maureen—your loving Caribbean calm helped us all stay sane this year. Heartfelt thanks to both of you.

CONTENTS

INTRODUCTION   xiii

one   Womenomics 101   1

two   What We Really Want   23

three   Redefining Success—It's All in Your Mind   47

four   Good-bye Guilt (and Hello No)   79

five   Lazy Like a Fox: Work Smarter Not Harder   109

six   Value Added: Redefine Your Value, Value Your Time   133

seven   Nine Rules to Negotiate Nirvana:
How to Change Your Whole Work Deal   161

eight   A Womenomics World   195

Epilogue   215

Endnotes   223

introduction

Erin clicks SEND *on her last e-mail of the day, stretches her legs, and checks her watch. Relief and anticipation flood through her. She's right on schedule— half an hour to pack up, grab a Diet Coke, and reach her son's baseball practice at four o'clock. She relishes these afternoons with him, and arrives at seven in the morning on Thursdays, just to be sure she'll be out the door on time. And then she often finishes up any remaining work she has left in the evenings—from home. A trade well worth the extra hours, Erin shrugs, as she gets her papers together. Her boss says he doesn't mind, as long as it's only once a week. She rubs her head. Did he seem put out last week when she reminded him she'd miss an afternoon meeting? She must be imagining that. Her work is stellar, after all. She's a rising star. Of course, she will have to endure the gauntlet of raised eyebrows from colleagues as she heads out, briefcase in hand, clearly leaving for the day. Her shoulders tense a bit as she grabs her keys.*

A shadow crosses her desk. Her boss, Michael, a friendly but exacting fifty-two-year-old, a top performer at the company, has something in his hand. Dread invades her stomach as the blue binder hits her desk. "Erin," he says, his voice urgent, excited even. "We've just been offered a shot at the Clearwater deal. Could you take a quick look, let me know your thoughts?" Erin stares up at him, frozen in frustration, as her mind plunges into that exquisite form of maternal torture: imagining the agony of a disappointed child. Can she say no? And then her ego kicks in. The Clearwater deal—she knows that project cold. It's the sort of work that gives her an adrenaline rush and would really burnish her reputation. Why does it feel that there are no good choices? It would be easy enough to go through the report a few hours from now, and e-mail her thoughts to Michael, but how will that look? Uninterested? Uncommitted? She begins to feel physically ill, as those familiar stress hormones kick in. Why does she feel so guilty, so powerless, so trapped?

Erin could be Mary, she could be Andrea, she could be Karen. She could be a sales rep, or a doctor, or an accountant. She could be in Houston, Minneapolis, New York. And that commitment to her son could be a visit with an elderly father, a marathon training session, or even a long-planned outing with friends.

Erin was us. She's probably you. But she doesn't have to be. Not anymore.

For years the two of us would often swap our own personal versions of the Erin experience—furtively at first—until it became clear we had a similar sensibility. We worried that anything that smacked of lack of ambition, of working but not always aiming for the pinnacle, just wouldn't be professionally correct. And so in an ironic twist on the old-boys network, we'd offer each other private advice on *turning down* plum jobs and *avoiding* tantalizing promotions that might upend the hard-won balance of our daily lives.

The more we talked, and then read, and then reported, the more we realized we were on to something much bigger than our own experiences. What we've uncovered is nothing short of a brewing workplace revolution. And it's a revolution, luckily for all of us, well-suited for any economy. Indeed tough economic times are ushering in the change even more quickly.

A few facts: the overwhelming majority of women are longing to kick down that dreaded corporate ladder, flee the 8 A.M.-to-day-care-closing dash, but at the same time hang on to some real status. We have had enough of the fifty- or sixty-hour workweeks, holidays that never get taken, the juggling and spinning and rushing. We know the solution isn't longer hours at day care or hiring more babysitters or asking our husbands to stay home. Because we're the ones who want more time—for our children, our parents, our communities, ourselves.

Most educated women don't want to quit work altogether, even if they could. We want to use our brains and be productive professionally, but we don't want to keep tearing at the fabric of our families or our lives outside of the workplace. We need to slow down. We *want* to slow down—to take a moment to thank the cashier at the grocery store, to indulge in banter with our neighbor, to occasionally handle ballet drop-off or make it to our book club. We want to be *in* our lives.

And frankly, we have the same desire for our work existence. We'd like to spend our time at work engaged in meaningful and fulfilling pursuits and grown-up interactions with colleagues—focused on results. We've had enough of worrying about punching a clock or ringing some macho bell to the tune of he-who-stays-in-the-office-longest slays the biggest mammoth.

The situation is so dire that a majority of us will opt, when asked, for *less* responsibility. We will trade duties, a title—even salary increases—for more time, freedom, and harmony. We don't want to quit—far from it—but *time* has become our new currency. Eighty-seven percent of the women in a recent study say they'd like a "better balance," or as we put it, more *sanity*, at work. (And are the other 13 percent being honest?)

It's an issue that now even has a champion in the White House. "It's always guilt-filled," Michelle Obama told Claire in an interview on the campaign trail. "Constant guilt surrounds working women and mothers no matter what you decide to do." The First Lady wants to put a national spotlight on the frustrating balancing act that so many women face, and which she herself had to master.

The pride of their working-class family, both she and her brother excelled at Princeton, and then she went on to Harvard Law School. Before her husband became president, Mrs. Obama had a thriving career, but since the birth of her daughters, she's made it plain she considers raising them her top priority. And she backed that up in her job choices—opting for flexibility over promotions. "No matter what decision you make at any point in time," she concluded, with an understanding shake of her head, "you feel like you should be doing more on the other end."

It's great to know we're not alone in our angst, but you'll feel even better when you learn that this uniquely female torture doesn't have to be yours, or any woman's. Not anymore. Why?

The scale of transformation roiling beneath the surface is immense. This is a moment in history when outside forces have aligned to create a profound upheaval in the world of work.

Another fact: women top every company's most wanted list.

We'll bet you had no idea just how essential you are. (Naturally that information isn't just handed out to the masses. That would give us too much leverage.) A treasure trove of remarkable new economic data plainly proves we have power like never before. And hard data is critical, because, after all, we're not going to get something from the business world just because we want it. We have to be valuable to the bottom line in order to force change. And are we ever. Why? Because businesses with more women in senior positions make more money. It's as straightforward and stunning as that.

The business world is changing in ways that call for more brain over brawn, and our more inclusive and constructive management style is in high demand. Again, this claim is not wishful thinking; you'll see the research. And when you do, it will make perfect sense. Our right-brain multitasking and problem-solving skills help us make good corporate decisions. And companies now understand that a woman's opinion about products is critical, since (as we all know) we do the bulk of the buying for our families. Throw in the fact that we've got more degrees than men do and that there is an approaching talent shortage, especially of college-educated workers, and anyone can do the math. We have never been hotter. And it helps, by the way, that our savvy youngers are fanning the flames, demanding more freedom than we've dared.

"I think it is about women, and in some ways, even more about Gen X and Gen Y," agrees Meg Whitman, the former CEO of eBay and a keen follower of business trends. "There's no question that workforces and workplaces are changing dramatically."

One more fact: Not only is all of this still relevant in a recession, but it's absolutely essential. Over and over again companies have told us that retention of *valuable* talent is key in tough economic periods, as is the need to get smart about how to accommodate employees.

"At times like this, if people believe they have control over their time and that the company has a good philosophy, it helps morale," says Cynthia Trudell, senior vice president and head of personnel at PepsiCo. "And remember you want the best and the brightest when you're going through difficult times."

So, what happens when you combine all that swooning over our gender with the fact that most of us want to avoid a grim robotic march to a chilly top? You've got the recipe for a mega-trend we call:

Womenomics (/wim'in·näm'iks/) n. **1.** Power. **2.** A movement that will get you the work life you really want. **3.** The powerful collision of two simple realities: a majority of women are demanding new rules of engagement at the very moment we've become *the* hot commodity in today's workplace.

Thanks to the heady new world of Womenomics, professional women can finally get what we really want. We can radically transform the way we work and the way we look at work, we can redefine success on our own terms. And we're not talking about doing more work for less money, thanks to some pseudoflexible schedule. No.

In ways they never would have done even five or six years ago, major companies are starting to adapt to our lifestyle demands. They finally understand we're not looking for a better company cafeteria, a free dinner after working late, or a fancy gym—all glittering handcuffs to keep us on the job. We want freedom—to make our own decisions, to control our own work lives. Our talent, experience, diligence, and commitment, they are coming to see, are more than fair trade.

In enlightened pockets of the working world, Womenomics is already happening. There are companies that allow you to choose from a menu of work options. There are part-time law partners who still get the big cases. There are company executives who work full time but who spend no more than thirty hours a week at their desks. There are accountants who get home at 3 P.M. every day but who stay firmly on the company fast track. And there are companies where you can work wherever and whenever you want, as long as you meet the bottom line. Technology and power and plain common sense are freeing us from that antiquated morning-to-evening prison in ways we could not have imagined a decade ago.

Though women are leading this charge for change, it will soon benefit the entire working world. Some firms are embracing this wave on their own; others need a gentle push, while the rest may need to be dragged into this new era. But they will all be there, and so will you.

Winning your professional liberation does demand a rethink—a fundamental reevaluation of what success really means. The push to that epiphany can be many things; for the two of us, as for many women, it was children. We both remember with vivid clarity our moments of insurrection.

KATTY   My route to professional enlightenment led straight through the U.S. Capitol. It was a gray, drizzly March afternoon. I was sitting on the steps of Congress, waiting to do a live report on the latest machinations of that illustrious elected body, when my phone rang.

I knew exactly who it was. I tried to ignore it.

It was my boss, offering me a job I didn't really want. Or rather, I really wanted the job—anchoring an evening news show—I just didn't want the hours that came with it.

The phone rang again—I still didn't pick up.

I knew I could do this job and do it well. I knew I'd have fun. I also knew with total conviction that I would be miserable if I did the job five days a week, which they were insisting on. I had reached a line in the sand. The job I currently had was also fun, reasonably well paid, and flexible enough to allow me enough time at home. I would do the new job four days a week or not at all. I was prepared to walk away.

Still, this was ridiculous. Here I was, a grown woman, afraid to pick up the phone. I answered. I told my boss about the four days and that line in the sand, I said I would of course be happy to help out and fill in when the new anchor was away but that I couldn't take the job under the terms they needed.

Then the executive did something I hadn't expected.

She said that she didn't want to have just a reputation for being family-friendly—she actually wanted to be family-friendly. She really wanted women with experience on air, and she really wanted me to do the job. If I could only do it on my timetable then she would talk to her bosses and recommend they accept my four-day-a-week proposition. And she did—and they did.

At that point my producer came screaming out of the Capitol—shouting that I was on air in five minutes. I did some rather dazed political analysis, and only when I was done did I take a breath and realize I had got it all.

CLAIRE   The fifth-floor executive suite at ABC News never fails to intimidate. The plush furniture. The hushed tones. The top executives all huddling, the occasional visitor imagines, to pass judgment about the network players.

This day, though, I was feeling somewhat more confident than usual. I had a reasonable request to outline, and I was bolstered by the fact that I didn't really care (much anyway) about the consequences. That attitude was years in the making, but it had finally arrived. Despite the last-minute nature of our business, I was now forty-three with two children, and I needed to be able to plan at least SOME aspects of my life. Holidays, for example, and travel.

I was sweating a bit, and my voice was starting to sound whiny. I dropped an octave, tried for polish, and wrapped up my plea. The female executive on the other side of the desk had long been my mentor, supporter, and friend. But I'd been sensing a growing exasperation at my struggle to change the rules. "That all makes sense, Claire," she said, "but it's just that. . ." She paused, searching for words. "Everyone else here jumps when we say jump," she explained. "You don't."

I knew if I were in a clichéd Wall Street movie this was where I would fire back: "I will jump! I will! How high?" But I didn't think I could play that role convincingly. Instead out popped, "I don't think I'm a jumper."

Ugh. I couldn't believe I'd said that. Then I shrugged, unhelpfully, as I berated myself and wondered how "nonjumper" would look on my résumé, and whether it was a condition that could be treated.

The executive looked down. I waited for the worst, but it didn't come. "We've told you we like your work," she finally said, sighing. "You are complicated, but we'll deal with it."

The sense of liberation I felt that day was profound. At last the truth about my life at this point was out in the open. I'm a complicated nonjumper. And I'm still employed. And more importantly, for the first time in years, I'd taken an enormous step toward defining my job according to my needs, instead of the other way around.

Dare we say it? Will we jinx our newfound harmony? These days there are moments when we actually feel as though we've carved out something close to "Having It All."

Remember that tantalizing, agonizing phrase coined by *Cosmo* doyenne Helen Gurley Brown? And then that unforgettable Enjoli perfume ad where a sultry brunette strips off her prim Wall Street suit as she sings about her abilities: "I can bring home the bacon, fry it up in a pan, and never ever let you forget you're a man?"

Well, that's not exactly the "All" we're talking about. That "All" was somebody else's vision—a distinctly masculine vision, if you think about it, on all fronts. And it's tripped us up for years. Even today's glum thinking about our choices is still a backlash against the old "All." The "mommy track" at work has been a lonely demoralizing road from which there's usually been no return. The path to the top has been paved by a few brave execs who've managed to squeeze in kids with considerable stress and against the odds. And many of the most educated women in the country have quit prestigious and powerful jobs after a handful of overstretched years and are now staying at home with their children. The pessimistic assumption is that we can't do both career and motherhood successfully. Well, we don't buy it.

When the term "Mommy Wars" entered our lexicon, we looked at each other, bemused. What wars? It didn't make sense to either of us. Women aren't battling one another based upon a mythical divide between working and nonworking mothers. Every single woman we know is far too busy sorting out her own path to have time left over to wage an ideological battle over whether working or not working is the Right Thing.

Most of us want to work—but on our terms, in ways that make it possible to have a life as well. *That's* the subject inspiring passion at lunches, in hallways, and around the watercooler.

"The *New* All"—that's what we like to call our aspirations, what we've managed to pull off. Over the years, the two of us worked out our priorities and professional lives so that we are neither tied to our desks nor our kitchens. We've taken unique routes, and there's one for every woman. Claire works for one company, with which she has negotiated her own flexible hours. Katty works for a few different organizations, which provides three different sources of income. She sees herself as a "consultant" to all of them, an arrangement that buys her flexibility and independence from all her employers. Neither work schedule is part of an "official" program anywhere, and we've had to steer through rocky territory to get there. We've had to redefine our own notions of success, ignore the judgments of others, and quite often make brutally hard career choices to get what we discovered we most wanted in this "New All"—*enough* professional success, balanced by time and freedom.

KATTY   I'm British but really more of a nomad. My dad was a diplomat whose job took us all over the world, so perhaps it's not surprising I ended up a journalist. My mother battled rigid diplomatic traditions and the demands of four children to carve out a portable career as a writer. Isn't it funny how we repeat those patterns? I always knew I wanted to work, I guess I learned it from her. I also knew instinctively that I didn't want a sixty-hour week and no time with my kids. I moved to Washington, D.C., from Tokyo in 1996, and since then I've worked part time, full time, and not at all. I've tried them all, and finally I've got a great setup where I work on average thirty hours a week as a TV reporter. Those other hours? I guard them fiercely for my own four children.

CLAIRE   I always knew I'd work. My father was a professor who never doubted our abilities. My mother was a small-town schoolteacher from Texas who quit her job when my sister and I were born. I'm not sure she regretted it, but almost every day she was alive she made it plain she wanted us to have meaningful careers, and be in charge of our own destinies. As a mother, she was wonderful, creative, loving—forever whipping up seven-layer cookies or papier-mâché dragon costumes. I remember reveling in knowing she was always there for me. I want that for my children, but I also want my career. In my twenties and early thirties, as a reporter with CNN in Moscow and Washington and around the world, and then covering the White House for NBC, I was childless and confident that a family would somehow just "fit in." My move to *Good Morning America* coincided with my first pregnancy, and suddenly my entire view of the world changed. My gut would clench every time an out-of-town assignment (which I used to live for) came up. It still does! Once I finally confronted my changed ambitions head-on, it wasn't simple for me or ABC, but the company has been remarkably open to helping me find a different role.

This book is not just our story. We've interviewed dozens of women and their employers across the country and across professions who've pulled off the same thing.

"I was so nervous. I couldn't believe after all my years and stature that I was going to ASK for a demotion," remembers Robin Ehlers, a sales manager with Pillsbury at the time, whose success convinced the company to say yes to her demands for a virtual office and who still decided to take a step down to spend more time with her children.

Sarah Slusser, a senior executive with a Virginia-based energy company, had a revelation just as she was about to move her family to New York. "The Wall Street offer seemed like a dream— but then I realized—it wasn't my dream." Instead she used her years of credit with her company to combine senior status with flexible hours and more time with her boys.

Womenomics is, at its very essence, a philosophical, even spiritual approach to getting things right. In work and in life. (And it's something the corporate world needs as much as we do these days.)

But get ready. This is not a gauzy, feel-good, candle-lighting manual. We're not going to advise you to rub peppermint scrub on your feet to "take care of yourself," or to make time for your herb-infused yoga. You'll have time for all of that *after* you adopt Womenomics, mind you, but that's not the solution. This is a hard-nosed system that will teach you, step by step, how to get professional freedom by capitalizing on the approaching wave of Womenomics.

We will help you find more time in your day by cutting your time at the office. We will help you shake the stress but keep the income and clout. We'll teach you how to come clean about what you really want, how to ignore what the traditional careerists say you want, and how to say no to what you don't want. You'll learn how to get rid of guilt, that useless female affliction. We'll show you how to get the most impact for your time by being strategic about which tasks you take on. We will hand you the tools for all of it—down to the specifics of how to unplug from technology or how to schedule appointments so they work for you.

This is not a parenting book. There are plenty of those. And you don't have to have screaming, knee-high people in your life to benefit from Womenomics. No—this is the path for all of us to find the time for fulfillment, whether it's for kids, ailing parents, marathon running, or even, as we found in one case, your beloved dog. We don't care what your time is for—we just know you need it. And this book teaches you how to uncover it. Younger women, we've noticed, are extremely passionate and intuitive about avoiding the mistakes we've made and are already searching for solutions. For those of you just starting out, we'll help you navigate the pitfalls. (And when you've finished this book, pass it along to the men in your life. They may not say it as loudly as we do, but they want this too and can learn from the way women are remaking the future.)

And, yes, not only is all of this still possible in a recession, but it may well be easier than ever. We'd argue, in fact, that a woman's desire and capacity for flexibility and her unique management skills could be the silver lining of this economic downturn. A number of employers are introducing alternative work schedules, furloughs, unpaid vacation time, and reduced schedules specifically in response to the economic situation. These firms see flexibility as a way to keep up morale and avoid mass layoffs. Companies of all sizes, including giants such as Dell, Honda, Nevada casinos, and the *Seattle Times*, are getting creative about cutting labor costs. They want to nip and tuck instead of slash.[1]

Because women do tend to value time as much as money, flexible schedules offer solutions women often welcome. One mother of three, recently placed on a mandated two-week furlough, said she quickly turned what seemed a "negative" into a "positive." By spreading the furlough out, she realized that she's gained a trial period for the four-day workweek she's been after and is secretly thrilled to have the extra time.

Moreover, it seems that the recession may be highlighting female management strengths even more clearly. At the World Economic Forum in Davos earlier this year, the buzz was that if Lehman Brothers had included some sisters or if the top investment banks had had more senior women making decisions, perhaps the economic crisis might have been averted. New research shows that men are prone to risk taking, while women make more cautious decisions at work. A study in France found that companies with more women in management positions did better during 2008—had higher profits—than those with fewer women. Luxury brand Hermes was the only large company listed on the French stock exchange whose share price actually rose last year (by 16.8 percent), and the firm also happens to have the second-largest feminized management of companies listed in the exchange (55 percent).

"Feminization of management seems to protect against financial crisis," says Michel Ferrary, professor of management at the CERAM Business School in France. "In conditions of high uncertainty, financial markets value companies that take fewer risks and are more stable."[2]

This good news in a bad economy can help you get what you want, even today. Remember: companies will always need key talent, but now they've got to get creative in figuring out how to retain and reward the employees they value, and, more than ever, they value women. You'll find you can ask for flexibility and new ways of working that might have been cold-shouldered last year. You'll discover once-dogmatic bosses suddenly channeling Bob Barker as they try to make deals. You'll soon understand what we've uncovered and what the smart managers already know: letting people work the way they want pays off. It increases productivity, saves on a host of infrastructure costs, and produces salary savings when employees are literally looking to work less. At a time when bonuses or raises might not be possible, handing out freedom instead not only makes loads of sense, it is also what many would prefer.

Above all, Womenomics is real, and realistic. It's literally news you can use to make your professional dreams come true. Most of us don't want to quit our careers or work the crazy hours it takes to be CEO. We're not fantasizing (much anyway) about being able to learn kickboxing in Japan or flamenco dancing in Argentina while conducting our work via laptop. Most of us like our roots and are committed to our families; we enjoy the comforts of home and the gratification of being respected for our accomplishments. Our core fantasies revolve around having emotionally richer and saner lives.

We are not alone; we just didn't realize it. We have the power to demand that companies adapt to us; we just didn't know it. We can negotiate for more of what we want; we just didn't know how to do it. With *Womenomics* you are in on the ground floor of this revolution. And when you have to put the book down keep it tucked in your trendy purse, your battered briefcase, or your cheese-stick-and-Cheerios-filled diaper bag. You'll find it empowering at the most unexpected moments.

womenomics 101

Once upon a time big bad corporations employed women because they were cheap, made good coffee, suggested diversity, and, let's face it, looked a heck of a lot better than most men. Times have changed. Forty years after professional women first stormed the corporate barricades, those same firms are looking at us and seeing dollar signs. They've discovered that women deliver profits, often in big numbers, and that we are very worth hanging on to.

This is not just wishful thinking. A whole host of business brains, from Michigan to Norway, have uncovered an "asset-to-estrogen" ratio, which suggests two things: more women at a company can mean more profit, and every company in the Western world would do well to treat their professional women properly.[3] It turns out that women are incredibly valuable *and* inconveniently expensive to replace.

Your company needs you more than you realize and quite possibly more than you need them. The numbers we are about to give you prove that. Ready to crunch? Don't worry, we'll talk big picture; this is not an economics thesis. But these studies are so startling that we thought you could benefit from an up-close look at just how much power you have.

Pink Profits

The wise people at Pepperdine University realized it would be a good idea to take a bit of the emotion out of the debate about whether women are useful workers and chuck in a good healthy dose of economic analysis instead. They conducted a massive nineteen-year survey of 215 Fortune 500 companies.[4] The Pepperdine professors wanted to find out if companies with more women in top positions did better or worse than companies with fewer women. And, being economists, by better or worse they meant more or less profitable. This is a hard numbers game, remember. Do women help companies make money or not?

The researchers surveyed these companies every year with a complicated formula worthy of all their PhDs. They added points according to how many and how senior the women in the company were. They then took three different measures of profitability, since different industries measure their profits in different ways.

The results are little short of revolutionary. By every measure of profitability—equity, revenue, and assets—Pepperdine's study found that companies with the best records for promoting women outperform the competition.

Indeed the companies with the very best records of promoting women beat the industry average by 116 percent in terms of equity, 46 percent in terms of revenue, and 41 percent in terms of assets. We're not economists, but even we can see that, cut it whichever way you like, women are good for profits. (Indeed, the study was called "Women in the Executive Suite Correlate to High Profits.")

Professor Roy Adler, who conducted the study, believes one explanation for the high women-to-profit ratio may be that the high-performing firms do well because their top executives make smart decisions. One of those smart decisions is cranking open that heavy executive suite door to admit more women—well-educated and critical talent.

Now that, we reckon, is power in your well-manicured hand.

Still not convinced? These findings are not an aberration.

At the University of California at Davis, the graduate school of management concluded in 2005 that companies with women in top leadership positions have "stronger relationships with customers and shareholders and a more diverse and profitable business."[5] The school concluded that "diversity of thought and experience in leadership is good business strategy." And that's the key—employing women is no longer a politically correct palliative to diversity. It is good business strategy.

The independent research organization Catalyst, which focuses on women in business, also conducted a study of 353 Fortune 500 companies in the late 1990s. They wanted to explore the link between gender diversity in top management teams and U.S. corporate financial performance. Catalyst, like Pepperdine, found that companies with the highest representation of women in senior management positions performed best. They had a higher return on equity and a higher total return to shareholders—higher by more than one-third.[6]

As journalists, when we start to read successive reports that come up with similar conclusions, we call it a story. When the results are this conclusive and this notable we may well even call it a headline.

As journalists we're also cautious. We can't say that diversity is the only reason companies with more women are doing better.

Clearly there could be other reasons too. But there is indisputably a pattern here.

"Companies that recruit, retain and advance women can tap into an increasingly educated and skilled segment of the talent pool," says the Catalyst study.

Let's look at that pool a bit. How much do you know about women and their talents? We were surprised.

In education:

What percentage of bachelor's degrees do women in the United States earn? 40 percent? 50 percent? No, try 57 percent. And what about the degree that really counts for professionals, the master's? Here too women are on top. Women earn 58 percent of all graduate degrees. Even in business, women are now over a third of all graduates.[7]

And at work:

Nearly half the American workforce is female and the recession means we'll soon be a majority.[8] Women in management? 46 percent. At the extreme heights, the numbers are thin but rising. Women's representation in the senior ranks of Fortune 500 companies grew from 10 percent in 1996 to 16 percent in 2002. That's more than a 50 percent increase in just six years.[9]

And this recognition of female business clout doesn't stop at America's shores. In Norway the government has become so convinced of the value of women in business that the minister of trade has demanded that 40 percent of any company board be women—not to appear politically correct, but to make their firms more competitive internationally.[10]

In Britain researchers at Cranfield University School of Management now publish an annual index they call the Female FTSE (the UK's DOW), which measures the progress of women in the country's top companies.[11] They too have found that companies with women on the executive management team outperform their less diverse competitors.

It's clear: a company "allowing" you to work the way you want isn't just doing you a favor; it's making a strategic decision. Businesses want employees who boost profits. And in a flat or faltering economy, value is even more important. Our strengths are all the more noticeable.

So next time you're sitting at your desk far too long, are missing soccer practice for the forty-third time, are dreading your child's face as you show up late, and are wondering whether it is finally getting to be too much and whether tomorrow is the day to hand in your resignation, don't despair. Stop. Take a deep breath and remember pink profits. You know the expression "Every good career woman is just one bad day away from quitting"? Well, it doesn't have to be true. You don't have to quit.

Tomorrow you can go to your boss and explain that you need more control over your schedule—you need a work life that means you won't miss soccer practice, or ballet, or your elderly mom's medical treatment, or whatever it is you need time for. There will be no forty-fourth time. And, your discovery of pink profits can help you feel confident when you have that conversation.

Take it from us, it works. Something funny happened to both of us as we researched this book. We both found we felt more sure of what we wanted and, more importantly, of our ability to get it. The knowledge that as professional women we are high performing allows us to be more high maintenance. Facts like these, and those to come, are awfully convenient things to have in your head as you set out to create the work life you want.

KATTY   When my second child was very young I got divorced and decided the kids needed me at home for a while. I told the BBC that I loved my job but needed to take a while to look after my toddlers. My professional women friends tut tutted, saying that I'd never get back in, that I couldn't afford to stop, that I'd fall off "the radar." And while I knew it was right for me to be home at that stage, my self-esteem really suffered and I worried that I might have given up any chance of a career for good. In the end the naysayers were wrong. I got back onto that radar, part time and freelance at first, then slowly and, after several hiccups, into the more full-time position I wanted. After a while I came to realize employers were keen to have a competent, experienced woman back on the job, even one with several kids and a three-year gap in her resume. All they really cared about was whether I could perform at the right cost, to the right level today. This simple (but critical) knowledge that you can structure your career the way you want, that you do have real power, can literally change your life.

Different—in a Good Way

The thing about opening that boardroom door to women is that firms aren't just expanding their talent pool at random; they are expanding it specifically to include *women*. And women, as we all know, are different from men. Different, it turns out, in very useful ways.

We know instinctively that women do business differently than men do. We can't help it. It is hardwired into our genes. For decades, though, women thought they had to be like men to get ahead. Our voices had to be louder, our emotions buried deeper, and our shoulders necessarily broader. (There has to be some reason for those hideous 1980s pads.) Think Margaret Thatcher—aka the Iron Lady.

Well, that gender-swapping style doesn't work for us, and thank goodness, because we are all better off as we are. Both better off and *better*. It is not just in romance novels that a little

yin goes well with the yang. Companies now realize they perform best when they have the right mix of male and female
management styles.

The Mars-versus-Venus school of leadership is well studied.
It will come as little surprise to all of you that women have a
style of management that is more open and more inclusive than
that of the other sex. We are more likely to encourage participation in meetings, and we tend to be more nurturing of subordinates. We prefer consensus to confrontation and empathy over
ego.

Speaking of ego, Harvard Business School has even done research showing female stars are more valuable than male stars.[12]
There is evidence that company superstars aren't very portable—they don't transfer very well and tend to perform less well
in their new firm than their old one. Unless a company can hire
the star and his whole team, it is likely that his megasalary will
be wasted, because the newly recruited star player has a hard
time building new relationships. However, early in 2008 Professor Boris Groysberg released research suggesting this second-
act rule doesn't apply to women.[13] Groysberg gathered data on
nearly a thousand Wall Street analysts and found that if women
shone at their last firm, then they will continue to shine just
as brightly at their next, even without their backup team. He
credited this to women's unique ability to build such good relationships with clients and peers that they can re-create those
networks wherever they go. It's just one indication of how wom-
en's natural social skills translate well in the business environment.

What's surprising really is that for so long women knew that
these qualities of inclusiveness, empathy, and a flexible approach
to problem solving were useful in our personal lives, marriages,
and friendships, but we failed to realize that they are also great
resources in our professional lives. They are needed more and

more in a business world that increasingly values right-brain empathy over left-brain number-crunching.

It's something Geraldine Laybourne, the founder and former CEO of the Oxygen Media Network and the former president of Nickelodeon, always instinctively understood, even if discussing it wasn't politically correct.

"I had been president of Nickelodeon for about four years, and people were astounded that I had taken it from a moribund nothing, to something great in four years," she remembers. Her higher-ups asked her to talk about her success at a conference. "So I made a speech about why I had succeeded, and it was called 'Because I am a Woman.' And you could have heard a pin drop in this place, and the women were aghast . . . I mean this is in the 1980s." She laughs. "Don't call attention to it, don't say you're different."

Across the Atlantic a group of British captains of industry and commerce got together to envisage the workplace of the future. The Chartered Management Institute jumped forward a decade to 2018 and, in the first report of its kind, predicted a workplace that is more fluid, more virtual, less office-bound. It is one where the demands for women's management skills will be stronger than ever.[14] The report said that as the social changes from the past thirty years really take hold, women will move into higher management positions because their skills will be essential to this new way of working. The CMI found that recruiters are looking for emotional intelligence and the ability to appreciate people's values as much as they are looking for technical competency.

But don't worry, you don't need to wait until 2018. Companies already understand they need you.

Dan McGinn is CEO of a consulting group in Arlington, Virginia. He's been in the business twenty years and used to only employ women on a traditional career path who worked fifty-hour weeks. "Women as men," he calls it. He's changed his mind. Radically. He's now a cheerleader for employing women on their time terms, something he says he'd never have done a decade ago. "About six or seven years ago I started to focus more on productivity and success and less on rigid rules. It dawned on me that there was this whole pool of talented women I was missing out on."

McGinn changed his thinking and then his business practice. "We're in a brain race—we win if we get the best brain power. And if you think that way, it gets you out of the box in your office and it gets you off the clock. It's not about location or time, it's about the best ideas, the best intellectual power. When you think that way, you immediately become a lot more flexible."

And it's not just that women are diligent and efficient. McGinn says they give him an outlook on his clients' needs that he just wouldn't get from men.

Until recently, the image of the ideal corporate leader was of someone who is independent, tough, and egocentric—think John Wayne meets Lee Iacocca. That might have worked back in an age when people had jobs for life and followed hierarchies with little question—when the workforce itself was largely male. But the new work environment demands a new type of leader. Technology and the expanded education of professionals have combined to shake up the old style of working. What it means is that a woman's perspective, our style, is now understood as unique and irreplaceable. Our bosses know it—though you probably had no idea.

CLAIRE   The TV business is by definition a group effort. We rely on
          the contributions of researchers, producers, reporters, camera
          people, and editors. Without any one of them the on-air
          product just won't happen, and without their enthusiastic

participation, it certainly won't be as good as it could be. But it's really the producer's job to manage all of these personalities. That was my starting role in the business, and it's one I found I had a knack for. I could keep a lot of balls in the air, soothe troubled egos, convince reluctant subjects to talk to us, and put a story together, all while keeping a firm order of priorities in my mind as we labored not to miss the deadline. I've wondered why, as I've studied our business over the last decade, so many of our talented producers are women. It wasn't until I started working on this book that I understood we have a natural talent for just this sort of management.

If you think for even a few minutes, you can probably come up with a handful of examples of what you bring to the table in your profession that men might not.

KATTY   As a journalist I find I cover news differently from my male colleagues. It's not just that as a woman I look different on TV. It's more fundamental than that. I identify and pursue important stories that my male counterparts wouldn't even glance at. Back in 2000 I was fascinated to read that professional women were leaving the workforce in large numbers. None of my male colleagues thought it was very interesting. But I saw it as a story that could have huge popular interest—and it did. Even hard-nosed political stories look different to me as a woman. In the early days of the 2008 presidential primaries I insisted we do a piece on why it had taken America so long to get even somewhat close to having a serious female candidate. My male editor was reluctant, but I pushed, and the story ended up being one of the best pieces we did. My value as a woman on air goes beyond tokenism or a desire to pretty up the picture, and my editors know that. Women add something different. Sometimes it's intangible, but switch one of us out for a man and the product won't be the same. This is definitely not limited to journalism or TV– it's true in businesses across the board. Whether you are in management, sales, marketing, research, medicine, law, or finance, you are valuable in part because of your female take on things. Now that we know this little, earth-shattering fact, it's time for us to use it.

The female knack of getting people to feel good about themselves means employees are likely to perform better and feel more committed to their employers. USC Professor Judy Rosener has found that women are more able to get subordinates to transform their own self-interest into the goals of the organization. She calls the leadership style "transformational" and "interactive." "Women encourage participation, share power and information, enhance other people's self-worth, and get others excited about their work," she explains.

Oh, and another reason working women and particularly working women with a compelling outside interest are great employees? We are beyond efficient. We would argue, in fact, that there is no one more efficient than a working mother. Remember the days before little Charlie and Isabel? The days when you'd be happy to doodle your way through interminable meetings, chat to your colleagues over coffee in the hallway, or hang out in the local bar for a post work cocktail? Well, add kids into your life, and suddenly your attitude to work changes, for the better.

Meetings? Short, sharp, and to the point. Doodling? Forget it, no time. Leisurely caffeine-fueled gossip sessions? No thanks. And as for drinks after work? Not unless our careers are seriously on the line. No. Postkids, we have become lean, mean, work machines. In and out of that office as fast as possible. And guess what's happened? We have cut our office hours and we do our jobs just as well (if not better) because we are hyper-focused.

Feminizing Ford— or the Secret Power of Being a Consumer

Here's yet another way female roles are changing to give us more power in the business world: we buy stuff, lots of it.

"At the same time that their managerial representation is growing, women also make and influence purchasing decisions," the research organization Catalyst finds. "In 2001, women earned almost $2 trillion of income in the United States."[15]

We like to shop and $2 trillion is a lot of spending money. As every marketer knows, with purchasing power come demands, and we want to buy from people who understand our tastes and needs. That means we want to buy from women—not just female salespeople, but also female designers, advertisers, and suppliers as well.

"As a result," Catalyst continues, "the company that leverages its female talent internally will be better able to develop products and services that could appeal to its external customers." That is economist-speak for: employ more women in senior positions and you will produce the types of cars, kitchens, and Caribbean holidays that women actually want to buy. Add in a senior female salesperson on your shop floor and your firm will do better still.

Here's a four-wheeled example of how changing consumer patterns are affecting entire industries.

We bet you didn't know that women now buy more cars than

men. Yes, that bastion of male influence is becoming a little softer.

In 2007 women broke the automobile halfway mark and bought 53 percent of all cars in the United States—and we influenced 85 percent of all car purchases.[16]

This is affecting the car industry as a whole, from the design to the sales floor. Just like men, we want performance, features, and design, but Ford has found that women want those things differently. For a start we want more safety features, more storage, and more convenience. Toyota has had huge success with female customers—60 percent of all of its passenger cars in the United States are bought by women. Their surveys have taught them that women appreciate practical changes, like grocery bag hooks in the trunks. Indeed, their focus groups reinforce classic, almost humorous gender differences. All of the women spent time inspecting the inside of the cars, looking at how comfortable they and their passengers would be, while the men examined the outside of the vehicles, commenting on design and horsepower.

But there are some things we do care about on the outside. This isn't a plug for the car industry, but get this—car designers have even changed the shape of their door handles to accommodate a woman's longer fingernails. Now, when car companies are worried about our nails getting chipped, we know we have power.

The feminization of the auto industry doesn't stop at door handles. Car makers are taking a woman's point of view into account when it comes to marketing too. That means they need to employ more professional women in all areas of the process—in marketing, advertising, PR, and even sales. And this is the power of Feminizing Ford. If companies have to employ women to appeal to women, those female employees start to have more clout. They can begin to dictate the way they work because they have a value to their companies that cannot be replaced by men.

The power of women as consumers is leaving its mark across industries. In the United States nearly half of all shareholders are women, half of all computers are bought by women, and women are responsible for 83 percent of all consumer purchases. Companies that supply goods and services to other companies or to governments say gender equality has become a competitive necessity. They also say they have lost contracts because sales teams have been too male-dominated.[17] Woe to any company that fails to recognize the power of the female purse and the pressing need to employ more of us in order to make sure they are producing, selling, and servicing goods in ways women genuinely need. And of course, in today's market, as companies scramble to get people buying again—who do you imagine is best suited to convince women to open their purses? Why, other women, of course.

It's basic. Women now have power in society as voters, decision makers, owners, and consumers. Companies that get a reputation as bad employers or bad producers for women risk jeopardizing their good names; in today's increasingly competitive, global economy, where news spreads at the click of a mouse, such a reputation can be a business disaster. Businesses that cling to outdated structures risk being out of business. Pretty soon, a lack of diversity becomes simply a risk not worth running.

Female Talent—
More Demand Than Supply

If all of this good news isn't enough to get your empowerment juices flowing, the Womenomics of demographics should do the trick. In the short term the U.S. economy may be experiencing a downturn, but it's the long term that has most employers wide-eyed. We are facing a talent shortage unlike anything in history. As baby boomers retire they will leave an enormous unfilled hole of talent, which means professional women will become more valuable than ever.

It's time for a few numbers again.

Baby boomers currently make up approximately one-third of the American workforce. Every year they are getting older and creeping ever closer to retirement. The first boomer was born on January 1, 1946; her name is Kathleen Casey-Kirschling. Now a New Jersey grandmother, Kathleen in 2008 became the first boomer to apply for Social Security benefits. But about eighty million more boomers will soon follow her.

The earnestly named Employment Policy Foundation estimates that by 2012 there will be a six-million-person gap between the number of college graduates and the number of people needed to cover job growth and replace retirees.[18] That gap will grow bigger not smaller as more boomers retire.

Hold on to your diplomas, the war for talent is about to begin. Yes—we are peace-loving mothers who spend a large part of our day discouraging our sons from staging the third world war with their light sabers—but this is one battle we don't mind joining.

Even if some labor is sent overseas and still more is transfigured into a hard drive, economists agree that the demand for top-end, smart workers will still outstrip supply.

Ten years after it produced its original, groundbreaking "War for Talent" survey, the consultant giant McKinsey & Co. has compiled a new report that shows companies are more desperate than ever to retain good employees.[19] In "Making Talent a Strategic Priority," McKinsey surveyed seventy-seven companies in America, Asia, and Europe across a spectrum of industries.

The consultants gathered information from six thousand managers and executives, and their conclusion was overwhelming. The most important corporate resource over the next twenty years will be talent: smart, sophisticated businesspeople who are technologically literate, globally astute, and operationally agile. "Talent has become more important than capital, strategy, or R & D," declares Ed Michaels of McKinsey. And as the demand for talent goes up, the supply of it will be going down.

Women already make up half the workforce, and our ranks are set to grow faster than those of men over the next ten years.[20] We outnumber men in such diverse occupations as accountancy, real estate, and health service management. But many women in their midthirties decide their stressful work hours are incompatible with raising a family, so they've been leaving mid- to senior-management positions in alarming numbers. All of which means there is an even greater talent shortage and an even larger pool of strong female talent waiting to be tapped.

Smart businesses know this. Lori Rodriguez is the marketing director for a small firm of accountants in Tampa, Florida. Now in her midfifties, Rodriguez says that when she started out the attitude was very different. "My generation went to work and just kept going on the treadmill. We didn't think we could ask for more flexibility, we were lucky to be there." But her firm, Kingery and Crouse, has now made flexible work arrangements a top priority.

Seventy percent of Kingery's employees work flexibly. Some perform a full-time job in four days. Others are paid by their hours. Some do a four-day job for four days' pay and are "definitely off" on the fifth day. Another mother gets home at three-thirty every day to be with her teenage daughter but has stayed on the company fast track.

Kingery's motives for allowing employees to work at different times and in different locations were entirely business driven;

they wanted to lure—and keep—good talent. "We implemented flexibility to attract really good talent from the local accountancy schools. It's also a great way to keep women with ten, fifteen years experience too. We have very satisfied employees. Our retention is high. Have we seen the benefits to the firm? No question about it. No question," says Ms. Rodriguez.

Think about it. The cost of replacing professional employees is going up, not down. The total cost of replacing a senior manager can be three times that person's salary.[21] According to some estimates, the cost of turnover for knowledge-based companies is even higher—a whopping 500 percent—and those are just the kinds of companies in which professional women tend to work.[22]

Organizations know they can save millions by reducing turnover. And the best way to do that is to hang on to the skilled people they already have.

This combination of an impending talent shortage and the high cost of replacement means firms are more prepared than they have ever been to make compromises to keep the good people they already have. That's you, by the way.

"Smart employers don't want to drive their employees so hard that they burn out. That is very expensive. The estimates of the cost of turnover keep going up, in large part because of this issue of the shrinking skilled labor force," says Anne Weisberg, a senior advisor to Deloitte & Touche's Women's Initiative.

Recession Proof

When we started writing this book, women friends and colleagues would say nervously, as they watched Wall Street struggle to stay afloat, "Wow, that's great news about our clout in the business world, but what happens in a recession? Doesn't that mean we all have to go back to keeping our noses to the grind-stone and feeling grateful for having any job at all? Won't bad economic times make it impossible to negotiate?"

Well, no. Do you see the baby boomers getting younger, or those Gen X and Yers suddenly getting older and more experienced overnight? The talent shortage is bigger, broader, and deeper than any one economic cycle. No economist can create a workforce out of thin air. Womenomics is here to stay.

For the accounting firm Kingery & Crouse, flexibility trumps recession. Would Kingery suddenly revert to more traditional nine-to-six work patterns? "No," said marketing director Lori Rodriguez, "flexibility is bigger than that."

Tom Mars, the executive vice president and chief administrative officer of Wal-Mart, a company known for its keen-eyed study of the future, says the trend is here to stay for all companies that don't want to become dinosaurs. "There's no doubt in my mind," he says, "that companies who don't recognize the need to change and adopt programs like this will in short order become another Eastman Kodak."

Moreover, he says, it makes even more sense now. "Look, in this sort of economy, it's the time to be smart," he explains. "We need to be productive and efficient. And working flexibly and being flexible is free—in many ways it's priceless."

So tougher economic times could be the perfect moment for your cash-strapped company to get creative about reducing its salary costs. If you can offer to save them 20 percent of your salary and benefits by shifting to a four-day week, they may leap at the chance in a way they didn't need to in boom times. Or even if you don't want to cut your hours, you might still be able to bargain for flexibility that you couldn't get before. During a recession your company may not be able to offer you a raise, but one easy way your company can compensate is to provide the option of working at home one day a week. "For some businesses that need to do so, offering flexible work opportunities to people who want them could enable them to cut staffing or overhead costs without having to make layoffs," notes a spokeswoman for the British swimwear company Bravissimo. "Our research shows that part-time and flexible workers are happier, more engaged with their work and therefore more likely to perform better and be more productive."[23]

Of course, you have to take your company's current business needs into account, and we will talk about the savviest ways to use this economic power later. Remember, women could well be the solution to both America's talent and labor shortages *and* to its short-term economic problems. Womenomics offers employers the possibility of higher productivity and even cost savings. It's not only "recession proof" but also "recession friendly."

Pink Means Power

The beauty of Womenomics is that it is not just an academic business trend. Far from it. The wave we are describing has a direct impact on your life. If, like us, you love work but love life too and want to find time for both, then the power of pink profits is the foundation on which to build your own New All.

We believe we have uncovered a valuable secret. Businesses have known for a while how useful and profitable women are. By sharing this privileged information with you here we've given you the tools to negotiate. You can now go to your firm with the knowledge of just how much they want to keep their good, professional women. That gives you a strong hand to play.

One of the women we interviewed for this book, Sarah Slusser (whom you'll get to know better later on), hit the spot about this newfound power of women to negotiate for not just the job positions we want but also for the lives we want.

"I think that there's definitely been an understanding that it's really important to have women in the workplace," Sarah told us. "That the women who have been there as long as I have, have so much to bring to the table that anything the company can work out with us is worth it. There's definitely that feeling. That our experience is so valuable to the company."

It's one of the great virtuous circles of Womenomics. You have power, so you feel more confident, so you come across as in control, and that is very attractive to an employer. You suddenly seem like an even hotter commodity because you project your power. Employers are far keener to accommodate someone who seems on top of themselves and their work— professionally and mentally. Pandering doesn't work; power does.

But what, exactly, does this mean for you? What does this power look like, on the ground or in the cubicle or even in the corner office? How are you supposed to wield it? When is the best time to squint your eyes and demand to live and work the way you've always really wanted? When and how do you have this conversation with your boss?

All of these are important questions, and each of them will be answered in the course of Womenomics. Our new power is only part of the story —think of it as a critical tool to help us get what we want. That turns out to be the heart of the revolution— figuring out what we want. As you'll learn in chapter 2, the roar from the trenches for a new way of working, for a New All, is almost deafening.

Once upon a time big bad companies treated women as pawns not princesses. As in all good fairy stories, the princess has triumphed, which, let's face it, doesn't really surprise us. Princesses, like most women, are very good at what they do.

news you can use

1. Companies that employ more women make more money. It's documented.

2. Your perspective and management style are hot.

3. We do most of the buying, so they now know they need us to do the selling.

4. A talent shortage looms, and women account for more than half of the educated workforce.

5. It's expensive to lose experienced, professional women, so businesses *will* compromise.

6. In a downturn, companies are looking for creative ways to cut labor costs without big layoffs. This could be the perfect time to negotiate for time.

what we really want

Right about now, juiced up on all of that power you didn't know you had, you probably feel like grabbing your bayonet and heading for the boardroom. Some of you may want to seize— finally— that CEO's chair, or grab other ruling positions. Most of us, though, are after something even more elusive—freedom, time, control. A sane work life.

It's something we've long been afraid to demand. Afraid because we didn't know we *could* demand it—we didn't know all that stuff about our market power. But also afraid because even discussing the subject seemed risky—we'd look like slackers for raising it. And afraid because of what the lack of discussion implies—that women of our sentiment must be few and far between.

Well—guess what? You are not alone. The X chromosome natives, in really really big numbers, are restless. All across America women are making radical decisions about their careers—rattling the traditional workforce structure, which just doesn't fit with our enlightened mind-set. Some are emboldened by an understanding of their increased power. Others don't even feel that power but have reached a breaking point and are forging ahead on their own. We are forcing our work to suit our lives, not our lives to suit our work. We're determined to craft a New All for a new era, a formula that relies on sanity and control over struggling and juggling.

Robin Ehlers was happily on the fast track, eager to work hard and move up. The thirty-eight-year-old sales representative traveled the country for thirteen years building client relationships and winning stellar reviews. She was on her way to the challenging management position she'd always wanted. But she had two young children, and it wasn't always easy to meet the demands of both her job and her children—day care drop-off was often at 5:30 A.M. She and her husband even decided to move the family from California to Kansas City at one point so they would be closer to the nurturing help of in-laws. Even then, the stress was a killer. "You've got so much work to do, and you feel like you're neglecting your family, and especially your child. I remember most days picking up the kids and being too exhausted to be a mom." But her life worked, she told herself. On paper anyway. Until she was home on maternity leave after the birth of her third child and had time to really examine her priorities.

> It just kind of hit me. I couldn't do this anymore. I could already imagine the daily struggle once I got back. So I did something I'd literally never imagined: I saw some opportunities that were at a much more manageable career level—but they were lower. I basically asked to take a step down. And today? I'm so blessed. I love what I do, and when I want to ramp back up, I think I can.

Wired for Sanity

French feminist Simone de Beauvoir could have really used the help of a few brain scans. "One is not born, but rather one becomes a woman," she valiantly postulated in 1949.[24] She thought she was defending her sex by asserting that our more masculine side was forced out of us by societal forces. She was right that women have spent much of their existence stripped of power, but she was wrong on the nature-versus-nurture argument. Sixty years later, we all know now it's pretty much Mars versus Venus from birth, and these days, according to science and scans and studies, it looks as though Venus is rising. Sure this is still politically sensitive stuff—the president of Harvard got dumped over his musings that women may have different strengths. But we think we're on safe ground: we're not saying different—we're saying better!

You see, we noticed something the intrepid researchers at the Families and Work Institute kept tripping across as they conducted survey after survey about what employees want. We women experience our jobs quite differently from the way men do. We think about the future. We anticipate consequences more. We spend more time mapping out the potentially *negative* impact of taking bigger assignments. We have much broader concerns about the way demanding jobs might disrupt connections to family and friends. The researchers knew they were on to something big, but they couldn't really figure out how to quantify it. Were women's different attitudes rooted in scientific differences or something less tangible?

We took the anomaly to some brainiacs and discovered that those female instincts, those thought patterns, are hardwired into the female DNA. And in a superior fashion, say some. "There is no question about it," says Dr. Fernando Miranda. "Women have much more sophisticated, much more evolved brains." Miranda, a neurologist who studies these differences, echoes what much of the cutting edge research shows—women really are able to use both sides of their brain more easily than men. Men live mostly on the left side, or in the analytical sphere. But our left and right sides, the analytical and emotional spheres, are more connected, which explains, for example, why women tend to feel more ambivalent about hard-charging careers than men do. We're constantly weighing two competing brain inputs. But it's the same process that makes us consensus builders and valuable employees! "I'd much rather hire women than men," Miranda confesses. "Men are wired to be oppositional by nature—more argumentative."

The science is even redirecting the most militant women's libbers. "Above all, the hormones women receive in the womb mean that, by nature, they do not want to be manic, one-dimensional workhorses who invest all their energies in one thing: their job (or hobby). Overall, they are less extreme than men," writes British journalist and ardent feminist Rosie Boycott, at the same time admitting those words would have made her blood boil a decade ago.[25]

Bottom line? We are constantly in touch with our emotions, even when we're not conscious of it, and we act accordingly. The pathways that let us focus on the future are simply more available. In addition, we're not distracted as much by testosterone, that hormone of instant gratification and domination, which, according to Miranda, not to mention thousands of years of life as we know it, can really muck things up.

No, we women are instead heavily under the influence of the hormonal secretions of the hypothalamus. That's the mysterious stuff that lets us smell a tiger at thirty feet and take him on if he threatens our young, or, in Womenomics-speak, lets us sniff out claustrophobic corporate culture from blocks away and jump ship if it threatens our family life. We viscerally understand from the start what the ladder represents—a grim, Kafkaesque climb that could cripple our relationships. Men, less neurologically able to project the future, focus more happily on the next rung.

Imagine the arguments Mme. de Beauvoir would have marshaled with that data.

What Women Want

So what were we thinking years ago, as we were drawn, lockstep, into those masculine, career-driven ranks? What made us defy our genes and bend our natural wills to the unnatural corporate structure? Certainly after centuries without power we were after status and achievement, not to mention the ability to make a difference and make some money. (Remember—we are only *partially* right-brain driven!) And we still have those desires. But we've also achieved a certain amount of wisdom from our years in the testosterone jungle—wisdom about what works for us and what doesn't. Even the once all-mighty motivator—the dollar—doesn't stack up against our new, more gratifying incentive—time. We have discovered we'd prefer a New All; a tapestry of family and work in which we define our own success in reasonable terms.

It's because we are, well, who we are, explains Kathleen Christensen of the Sloan Foundation, one of the biggest funders of studies on families and the workplace. "But it's not about the tasks, the cooking and the shopping," she says. Christensen has actually coined a new phrase for the modern women's role in family life: the meaning makers. "It's the women who basically cultivate and sustain the rituals in the family. Whether it's when a child loses a tooth, birthday parties, or major family celebrations, it's the women who see that as what they *want* to do."

CLAIRE   I somehow always imagined that I and my husband, a thoroughly spectacular and modern guy, would simply split child-rearing duties. I envisioned some sort of postmodern utopia, in which we both worked, but both made equal career "sacrifices" in order to be home with our yet to be conceived child. It would clearly just be a matter of scheduling. Needless to say, reality intruded in an unruly but ultimately genius fashion. About eight months after our son Hugo was born, I was struggling with the unpredictable demands of my work. After getting another last-minute call to come to New York for an assignment, I spent an angst-ridden few weeks. Should we hire a second nanny? Should I keep pushing my husband to carve more time out of his schedule to be home? It finally hit me. I was on the floor with Hugo, who was, as always, chortling as he tried to eat his toes, when I suddenly understood that this was bigger than a scheduling problem. It wasn't about more help, or even my husband's participation. I wanted the luxury, the joys, of time with my son. Even if my husband were home full time, I could see that wasn't the solution. I wanted— and needed— that balance in my life. It was a liberating, almost euphoric realization. I had to sort things out with my company.

So—let's get back to the hard numbers again, because these will surprise you as much as the stats about your power.

Work-life conflict is the top factor cited when "high-potential, high-talent" women leave their jobs. A Harvard Business School study conducted by Myra Hart found that 62 percent of the school's female graduates with more than one child were either

not working, or working part time just five years after gradua-
tion.[26] Lack of balance is what pushes us to the brink of quitting.

In survey after survey, flexibility—work-life control—is essential, say women, to our professional satisfaction. It's ranked
right up there with compensation. Four out of five of us say we
need more flexibility at work, according to the Family and Work
Institute.[27] Ten years ago 48 percent of working women surveyed
thought part-time work was the answer. In 2007, 60 percent of
us now say we'd prefer to work part time. And companies barely
have to dig to get this information out of their high-heeled
masses.

In Richmond, Virginia, Capital One had its eyes opened in
2003 to this growing demand. The financial services company
surveyed its female associates to find out what was really critical
in their work lives. Overwhelmingly the answer they got back
was flexibility. And the demand for it increased the more senior
the women became. "People said 'I need to be able to go and
see a soccer game or I need to go and do what I need to do,'"
says Judy Pahren, director of human resources for Capitol One.
"In fact we saw it across our entire workforce, not just with
women."[28]

And when General Mills decided to check in with its female
workforce recently, it asked which factor women thought was
most important in bringing more balance to their lives: outside
help (someone to do grocery shopping, yard work, etc.), a more
flexible schedule, or a shorter commute. Flexibility trumped the
other categories.[29] As a result, 53 percent of the women said a
flexible schedule was the key to making their lives better. Fully
61 percent said flexible work arrangements were critical to *con-
tinuing to work at the company*.

But here's the rub—most women don't think they get enough
support for flexibility where they work and worry that if they do
work flexibly it will make them appear less committed.

The Downshift

Look—having been shoehorned into an inhospitable, male-created work environment for all these years, it should be no surprise that our attitude toward work is so conflicted. But the real headline isn't that women are quitting in droves, as was the big news ten years ago. It's how much we're modifying our professional goals and work habits in order to *stay* in the workplace.

A watershed Family and Work Institute study put in bold what until recently sounded sacrilegious: women often don't want that promotion. Most of us are happy where we are, thank you very much. In 1992, 57 percent of all college-educated women said they wanted to move to jobs with more responsibility. (We could hardly admit otherwise—weren't we all *supposed* to want that?) Well, ten years later, only 36 percent of us wanted to take on more responsibility. And in 2007, it was down again—only 28 percent of us want more responsibility.[30] This thirty-point drop in fifteen years shows that 59 percent of us don't want another ounce of work or worry on our desks, no matter the reward.[31] Whether we're finally coming clean, or we've simply learned the perils of top jobs (or some combination of the two), most women clearly don't aspire to make that straight climb to the summit anymore.

And this downshift in career ambitions is just as true for the top dogs among us. The same Family and Work Institute social scientists picked out ten top-tier companies (think IBM, Citicorp) and talked with the top one hundred women in leadership positions at those firms. They kept after them for weeks, determined to get an accurate read. In the end, one third of those high-flying women admitted they'd voluntarily scaled back their career aspirations. Why? Not because they weren't up to the job—but because the sacrifices they would have to make in their personal lives were just too great.

In her twenties, Christine Heenan could clock the hours with the best of them. As a senior policy analyst in the Clinton White House, the long days, the challenge, even the stress were challenges she was happy to take on. "I loved being in the office at 7, working with smart, fast thinking people till 10 at night, going out after work, talking about work, and getting up and doing it again."

In 1995 she moved to Rhode Island, where she took on another challenge—head of government and community relations at Brown University. It was slower than the White House and there were days when she missed the old pace. Until she got a wake-up call, literally, hours after her first child was born.

"I got a call from my boss in my hospital room as I was holding the baby! There was a major thing happening at the university and she needed to talk to me about it. I told her, 'There's a doctor walking into the room, I'll have to call you back.' And she said 'All right. Well, try to call me by 10 A.M.'"

In retrospect what shocks Christine more than that request was her own response.

"I said, 'Okay'!" remembers Christine, chagrined. "If I look back, it's one of the conversations I would most love to have a do-over on, and say. . .'I'll call you when and *if* I can.'"

A few years later, after trying to work "flexibly" at the university, and with a second child in her family, Christine quit to start her own company, a company where she offered her employees the same freedom she gives herself.

"Plateauing" is what Wharton Business School calls this growing lack of appetite for the climb. "Women are no longer willing to step into the 'high-potential' pool of employees in part because they want to be sure they have time for their families," explains Monica McGrath, a professor at Wharton. "These women aren't lacking in ambition and they want to make a difference in their jobs. It's a question of 'how much more responsibility can I take on.' "

Women simply don't have linear career trajectories anymore. Cathleen Benko and Anne Weisberg, executives with financial consultants Deloitte and Touche, say that's exactly what prompted them to craft a groundbreaking program called Mass Career Customization at Deloitte. It allows all employees to easily adjust the pace and flexibility of their careers over time. "Women have noncontinuous careers. And if we hire twelve thousand people a year in the United States alone, not to mention globally, and many of them are women, that matters," says Benko. They say the ladder construct is out, *lattice* is in, for men and women. "We saw that the general trend line was more sideways than straight up, even for men, and even if you are the chairman of Deloitte."

Of course the fact that most of us haven't been able to take advantage of programs like that in recent years is why we've fled to smaller firms and the start-up market in search of friendlier terrain. Nearly *half* of all privately held U.S. businesses are now owned by women.[32]

Bottom line? Many women have to work, and most of us want to work. We enjoy being part of the challenging, captivating grown-up world. Even many of those who've quit altogether, unable to strike a reasonable deal to stay on the job, want back in. But Wharton recently followed a group of women who left and wanted to get back in and found that half of them reported the experience frustrating, and 18 percent found it depressing. We *so* don't need frustrated or depressing. We've got more than enough challenge in our emotional lives. What we do need to do is renegotiate the rules, reset the playing field, and get off that damn ladder, which, as it turns out, is not very stable anyhow.

The Ladder— It Is a' Crumbling

Even without your iPod you can hear echoes of Bob Dylan around every watercooler these days. The hot currency in office boasting sessions is quickly moving from the number of power breakfasts under your belt to the number of school plays you've managed to make. Women may be driving this workplace revolution, but make no mistake, *men* are realizing the benefits of flexibility too. We are simply the canary in the corporate mine.

At Capitol One Judy Pahren saw flexibility was no longer just a "women's initiative" when they did a follow-up to their survey and included the whole company. "We realized that flexibility was actually a need across our entire associate base. We had thought that maybe it was gender-based, but it was actually true of the men who worked here too," said Pahren. A few months later, the Flexible Work Arrangements program was moved out of the women's initiative and implemented for the whole company.

And no wonder—America is changing. "We are very much a time-famished nation. People want more control over their time," says Kathleen Christensen of the Sloan Foundation.

look at these stats:

78 percent of couples in this country are dual-income earners.

63 percent of us believe we don't have enough time for our spouses or partners.[33]

74 percent of us say we don't have enough time for our children.[34]

35 percent of adults are putting significant time toward caring for an elder relative.[35]

bottom line?

Half of us want fewer hours.[36]

Half of us would change our schedules.[37]

More than half would trade money for a day off.[38]

Three-quarters of us want flexible work options.[39]

Not a very satisfied group! It simply isn't our fathers' work-place anymore. More and more workers of *both* sexes are willing to scale back their career goals, according to Family and Work Institute data.

Many of us certainly see that at home.

"My husband is absolutely as concerned as I am about family time," says Robin Ehlers. "He runs his own business, so he's lucky, but he's always arranging his schedule to take three-day weekends for sports events, or even big chunks of the summer off to be with the kids. And I don't even bug him or nag him or ask him to do it!" she laughs.

"Reduced aspirations does not mean employees are not talented or good at what they do," explains Lois Backon of the Family and Work Institute. "Most do want to feel engaged by their jobs. But in focus groups they also say things like 'I need to make these choices because my family is a priority' or 'I need to make these choices to make my life work.'"

Why the changing priorities? Burnout is key, say experts, and the fact that companies, even though they still long to discipline us, can't really be decent father figures anymore. Benefits, pensions, other perks and protections are almost all a thing of the past. Not to mention job security, particularly in a downturn. Americans no longer believe they will spend a career at one shop, and they are right. The average American will hold ten different jobs over his or her lifetime.[40]

With the insecurity of that new mobility comes an unexpected benefit—more freedom. And the fact that we don't stay in one place for forty years anymore gives us enormous latitude to move sideways, backward, in and out—to define our own paths. We're looking for our security and fulfillment and confidence elsewhere. Our employer's definition of success is becoming meaningless, even suspect.

But—time for another reality check. We may want more freedom, but we're still scared. We long to embrace this new mindset, but we're worried about the consequences. Almost half of working parents believe their jobs might be in jeopardy if they work flexibly, especially now.[41] Not so, however, for the younger revolutionaries.[42]

Oliver Phillips, a partner at Brunswick Group, a strategic communications firm that advises a range of corporate clients, says younger employees are starting to measure success with a new yardstick. "The millennials are influencing expectations for the entire workforce."

The Naturals: Gens X, Y, and Z

If we're increasingly frustrated by the sixty-hour office week, the next generation has no interest in it at all.

When it comes to demanding freedom from the office grind, these guys are the power players. Because while *we've* learned it the hard way and are still racked with guilt about our choices, the younger generations just get it instinctively. It's as natural as texting and interacting on Facebook. Family and personal lives are critical for them. Old-fashioned pressure-cooker work environments send them screaming. They want to create unique, nontraditional career paths so that they can achieve all their life goals. They are impressively confident about their priorities, and they won't settle for anything less than liberation.

"Generations X and Y do have a very strong work ethic, but they want more balance—a satisfying work and personal life. And that is not just the women," notes Kathleen Christensen.

Remember, these alphabet-enders have grown up amid significant economic turbulence: the dot-com boom and bust, labor force shake-ups, corporate greed scandals, and the credit collapse. Coming of age in the era of 9/11 has clearly affected their priorities. They were raised by boomer parents who gave them self-esteem and a desire to have an impact. Consultant Bruce Tulgan, who helps companies work with younger generations, quips, "They are going to be the most high-performing civic-minded workforce in the history of the world, but they are also going to be the most high-maintenance workforce in the history of the world."

"Generation Y is completely untethered. They've been utilizing technology for years, so when they get into the work environment and they're a little more chained to their desk and to desktop computers, they don't know what to do," explains Cali Ressler, one of the cofounders of a radically flexible work program at retail giant Best Buy. "So rather than try to get them to conform to rules and guidelines from the 1950s, we should listen to them, and let them lead the way for what this future will look like."

Indeed these are the folks truly forcing corporations to think change—or risk having no workforce to take our place. Gen X and Gen Y together are smaller than the boomer crowd, and their very scarcity drives up their value. To employers looking at a labor shortage, their wants and needs are critical. The War for Talent survey puts it bluntly: "These workers demand more flexibility, meaningful jobs, professional freedom, higher rewards and a better work-life balance than older employees do. Companies face a rate of high attrition if their expectations aren't met."

Young women are especially focused on a well-rounded existence. A University of Michigan and Catalyst study discovered that many of the country's brainiest women are actively avoiding business school, their future-focused gaze honing in on the fact they won't be able to balance work and home life in the corporate world.[43] Concerned about business schools' inability to recruit some of the most talented women in the country, Wharton Business School makes a point of examining, in their program, how women can navigate the workforce in a savvy and family-friendly way. They know it's a subject the students want to discuss. "These women, now twenty-seven, twenty-eight, twenty-nine, are saying 'I have an MBA, and maybe it's going to be a problem,'" says Wharton's Monica McGrath.

Critical Mass

So what do you get when you have a workforce full of talented women who finally understand that what they want is to work differently, a substantial percentage of men who are starting to see they'd like the same thing, a much-in-demand younger generation that won't be tied down, a looming talent shortage, and, most important, a staggering increase in the value of women in the marketplace? An explosive chain reaction. And what's so remarkable about the process is that the change isn't just coming in a slow wave, as savvy businesses start to open up their minds and company policies. It's also coming in forceful ripples, as *individual women everywhere*—newly empowered and doggedly determined—negotiate for their New All. Every individual success and every act of confrontation chips away at the antiquated structure and adds to the momentum.

At the top end, there are victories like that of Brenda Barnes, the CEO of Sara Lee Corporation since 2004. Barnes quit her job as President and CEO of PepsiCo's North America operation in 1998 to raise her three children. At the time she was wildly criticized for hardening the glass ceiling. Now, kids in college, she's managed to become the nation's most high-profile, high-achieving on-ramper.

"Today's business world, where work can be done anywhere at any time, calls for a flexible environment that provides the opportunity for work-life balance," Barnes explains. "This doesn't mean employees work less; instead it means empowering employees to do their work on a schedule that works for them. So, if they want to work from their kitchen table at 3 A.M., as long as the work gets done, who cares when or where they are doing it? Companies need to recognize that this kind of flexibility offers employees the ability to manage and balance their own careers and lives, which in turn improves productivity and employee morale."

And, by the way, Barnes is working hard to be sure others can have the opportunity for fulfillment that she had. Sara Lee offers a multitude of flexible work options, and Barnes has also launched a program called Returnships. It's aimed at midcareer professionals who've been out of the workforce for a number of years, and offers them the chance to retool and retrain, with an eye toward a permanent, and probably flexible, job.

OK—maybe most of us aren't going to be able to quit a CEO job and then get another, but the fact that it's been done helps us all. And there are terrific, satisfying, and life-changing battles to be won that are well within reach. Robin Ehlers, now a sales rep for General Mills, works a full-time job based almost entirely out of her home, with only occasional travel. But negotiating this work life that works for her did not happen without a struggle. "After I moved down in status at Pillsbury, so that I could travel less and have a more manageable schedule, I was still working from the office," she explains. "I was trying to get my office moved to home and there was no way my boss was going to let me, but to me it just didn't make any sense in the world. I can remember kind of having a breakdown, and just thinking 'I just have to be at home. I can't waste the time on my commute when I could be with my new baby.'"

All of her work was by phone and computer with customers in other cities, and she felt she'd be equally, if not more, efficient at home. Her boss wanted everyone together, although "none of us even worked on the same team and we had plenty of opportunities to interact."

Finally, thanks to Robin's persistence—and a director who arrived and wanted her office space—her boss changed his mind. She got her deal, and when General Mills bought Pillsbury, managers saw no reason to change it. (Indeed, luckily for her, she's now at a company that truly encourages flexible work arrangements. General Mills gets high marks from its female employees.) Robin's negotiation, seemingly random and one-off, and the negotiations of millions of women like her, are having a collective impact by tearing down the old hierarchy brick by brick. But the savviest companies aren't waiting for disgruntled women to do the work; they are trying to do the demolition themselves.

Creative, manageable work programs are taking root all around the country—even in once-inhospitable corporate climates. Here's just a taste from the Family and Work Institute's list of recent award winners—you'll read about many more throughout the book.

- The Continental Airlines' reservations department in Houston has managed to keep its annual turnover to 5 percent—in an industry that has a 40 percent turnover rate. How? They let six hundred reservations agents work from home, which the mayor also appreciates as he tries to battle traffic congestion. And a quarter of the staff gets an extra day off a week on a rotating basis.

- Kay/Bassman International, a recruiting firm in Plano, Texas, offers the opposite of standard benefits. Each employee simply asks for what they need—to be home with children in the afternoon; to work via laptop—and in almost every case, the request is granted. CEO Jeff Kayle says humane treatment gets productivity results back to him in spades.

- The KPMG accounting firm offers their staff work-compressed workweeks, flexible hours, telecommuting, job sharing, or even reduced workloads. And workaholics beware: the firm has implemented wellness scorecards to find out whether someone is working too hard, or missing vacation. If so, supervisors are in touch to urge a slowdown! Oh, and how about eight weeks of fully paid maternity leave, even for adoptive parents? And two-thirds pay if you need more time.

- Chapman and Cutler, a midsize law firm in Chicago, started a two-tier pay scale in September. Hard-chargers who bill 2000 hours a year are paid top dollar. For those who prefer to slow down and see their families and friends, they can bill 1800 hours and earn less. *More than half of the associates chose the reduced schedule.*

Companies everywhere are starting to retool; they have no choice. "The one-size-fits-all workplace doesn't work," explains Kathleen Christensen. "The idea that you will work full time year in and year out, that you will be on a career trajectory that is a straight line, is vanishing. Employees increasingly feel more entitled to say 'I need and I want to work in a certain way.' "

A Win-Win

Here's the bottom-line bonus about all of these changes. Bowing to our demands makes business sense not just because companies need to keep us, but also because we become more productive employees. The unintended consequence took Capitol One by surprise. "People in the workforce have specific needs, and if they feel like you're going to work with them on those needs you can attract people and you can retain your best performers, which is probably the place we actually started thinking about this," admits the company's senior vice president Judy Pahren. "But then we found a much larger benefit. What we actually found is that it made people more productive. We discovered that this really helps productivity and job satisfaction at the same time."

Across the Atlantic in Britain, the Cranfield Univeristy School of Management conducted a two-year study with seven blue chip firms, including KPMG, Microsoft, and Pfizer (no fuzzy firms these) to measure the business impact of allowing employees to work on alternative schedules: [44]

- The majority of flexible workers increased the productivity of their performance, both in terms of the quantity and the quality of their work.

- The majority of employees said they were less stressed with a schedule they could control and they were more productive.

- Employees working flexibly were found to be more committed and more satisfied.

- The alternative work schedules were found to make the companies more competitive.

It seems pretty obvious, doesn't it? Employees who have the time to contribute to their communities, and who are heavily involved with their families, are actually better employees. We are indeed more committed and more productive and more loyal.

Certainly Geraldine Laybourne, who ran Nickelodeon and then the Oxygen network, didn't need any studies to show her that. Over lunch in a corner office high above Manhattan's East Side, she explained she was constantly experimenting with work practices, even decades ago, to encourage motivation, innovation, and loyalty.

"I had one guy in marketing who I thought was having trouble concentrating on big ideas. He was just coming in, spending terrible hours, and not producing," she remembers. "I told him he had to stay home on Fridays. 'You have to stay home and think. You cannot come in on Fridays!' " she told him, laughing. "So there were a lot of kooky things we did."

And at Oxygen, years later, she could finally create with utter ease the environment that nurtured the handpicked female talent she thought was critical to the company's success.

"We liked to hear about the kids. If you had to go to a play, you didn't have to hide that." She shrugs. "At one point at Oxygen we had twenty-four babies—twenty-four vice presidents out on maternity leave at the same time. And we had two senior vice presidents who were part time."

You can probably think of a moment when you've been so well treated at work you were inspired to do even more.

KATTY   I recently renegotiated my job at the BBC. A new boss arrived from an American network to shake up our evening news. The job I was offered was less prestigious than my previous job, and I was of two minds about whether to take it at all. I had a couple of other offers so was in the luxurious position of being able to walk away if I didn't get the terms I needed. It's fair to say I was a disgruntled employee! So I went into the meeting pretty militant; I would work flexibly or not at all. My specific condition was that if I wasn't needed on air for that evening's show, I wouldn't go in to the office that day. I expected at the very minimum a mutter of resistance—but to my surprise, I didn't even get a silent raised eyebrow. "That's fine," he said. And he kept to his word. No appearance on air, no appearance in the office. But here's what's interesting, and what I hadn't really anticipated: it's a freedom I am so grateful for that when I am needed I happily put in the extra effort. I win and the program wins."

We've all heard those stories about women who sneak out of work in a blizzard to go to the school play but leave their coats hanging over their chair in the office so their boss won't realize they've left the building. It's tragic how pathetic the tyranny of the office can be. We slip out anyway, but we resent our employers for it. It is far better to allow people freedom, and win their gratitude, not their resentment.

The Power of One

You might be thinking: these are great statistics on women, fascinating new trends going on in the workplace, and inspiring examples of a whole lot of individual women who are making concrete changes. But how can I really benefit from all of that?

The demographics, trends, statistics, and stories certainly don't amount to much if they remain unconnected to your life, your job, your level of day-to-day satisfaction.

Helping you make that connection is fundamental to Womenomics. And the first step, explains our former White House communications adviser, Christine Heenan, is to reexamine your priorities.

"I can say to myself I can wait until I'm 55 to try to learn piano," she said. "I can't say to my 8-year-old 'Would you mind starting the first day of school again because I didn't do it right the first time? I missed all of your games, so how about you be 8 again and I'll come this time?' It just doesn't work that way."

The rest of this book is devoted to helping you unearth *your* priorities, and then completely change your life at work and at home. You will have time, satisfaction, sanity. And as you make those changes and choices, know that you, as an individual woman, are contributing to a revolution that will carve out new possibilities—a New All—for all of us today, and for generations to come.

news you can use

1. You are not alone. Time is the new currency for all savvy women.

2. Even men want more of a life.

3. Watch your "youngers." They won't work any other way.

4. You may face a still rigid workplace, but you are on the right side of history.

5. Enlightened companies are already making work work better.

6. Balance makes you a better employee and human being.

THREE

redefining success—
it's all in your mind

Womenomics in your own life begins by taking all of the groundbreaking information from chapters 1 and 2—our business clout and our mass frustration at being boxed in—and using it to redefine success. We want to show you how to see your value through a whole different lens. We want you to work less but achieve more and live better. And, no, it's not a pipe dream. It's remarkably possible. We want to make sure that you go through such a profound mental shift that once you put down this book you will never again see achievement as hours in the seat, rungs on the ladder, and a fancy business title. It's all too easy to be influenced by other people's perceptions of what you should do. We're going to teach you to carve out a whole new, more satisfying path and write your own rules for success.

Stephanie Hampton was the public face of the hotel franchise giant Marriott International. As spokesperson, her job involved managing the public image of a megacorporation through a nonstop flow of communication with news outlets and industry journalists covering the company. For years Stephanie was basically on call, working ten- or even twelve-hour days and not stopping when the weekend finally arrived. Stephanie's talents and unceasing dedication didn't go unnoticed. After more than a decade of intense work, Marriott executives came to value her as an important part of the company. The corporate ladder that she'd been eyeing for years now seemed more like a cushy executive elevator that Marriott management was politely holding open for her. But one day something happened that fundamentally changed Stephanie's attitude to work.

"I had my annual performance review. I had spent the last year working very long hours, trying to do it all. But for the first time in my career I didn't get the top rating. I was doing well, but not perfect! And somehow it led to my "ah-ha" moment, as Oprah says. And I thought, 'Why am I killing myself?' I just had this moment and I thought, 'There's more to life than work.'"

For Stephanie, that mental reevaluation produced a very practical change in her life.

"I thought, 'You know what, I want to have children. I don't want to be fifty or sixty and look back and think all I did was work.' And that's when, for the first time, I actually put some parameters around the hours that I worked. And then once I really did that, I was able to get pregnant because I had been trying to conceive for a while but I was too stressed-out."

Stephanie chilled out at work, conceived, had her first child, and then got pregnant with her second. It was at the retirement party for Stephanie's boss—the executive vice president for communications—that Stephanie was reminded that a few years earlier she'd said that one day she'd have the top job. "Do you still want it?" she was asked. Stephanie didn't need to think twice. She wouldn't rule it out forever, but right now it was definitely not on her radar. "Ohhh, no." She almost shuddered.

With young children in the house, the demands of her current position were already enough. "Your priorities in life change, and I'm so glad that they did."

In the political minefield that is the female career track, Stephanie's realization is sometimes seen as controversial. "How can she possibly admit to not wanting the very top?" some feminists cry in horror. But we suspect that Stephanie is simply voicing what so many millions of career women are feeling: We actually *don't* want to make it to the very top of the ladder if it costs us so much else in our lives. We realize the price of not aiming for the very top may well be not getting to the very top. Or that it might take a lot longer. But that's fine with most of us.

It can be a frightening personal confrontation with your ego, but once it's done, new vistas open up. Like Stephanie, you too probably realize that what you have isn't what you really want: a job that doesn't leave you so stressed-out that you have no life, a job that doesn't demand so much you find yourself drawn inevitably to the brink of that agonizing choice of career or kids, where kids usually win. So here's where we get to the nitty-gritty and explain how you can actually get this sane fit. Watch as all that business theory, all those numbers and surveys, get put into practice to transform your day-to-day life.

There are two parts to this process. The first is mental. The second is practical. And no, sorry, you can't skip straight to chapters 5, 6, and 7 and get the quick fix. You really do have to go through the mental adjustment. Without it, you won't be able to take the practical steps necessary to change your life.

How critical is it? Run through a situation that will feel familiar. We've all been there.

Pre-Womenomics Workplace Scenario

You're sitting in your office after a long day of work and somehow you managed to get everything done, and done well. You're tired, hungry, and just aching to go home. But you can't: your boss is still there, and to leave while she (or he) is still sitting in the office feels like some sort of foul that could get you thrown out of the game—because you are playing by someone else's rules. So you sit around, wasting time, growing more exhausted, staring blankly at your computer screen until the boss takes off. Maybe you get a "Oh, you're still here?" from your boss. Maybe not.

Post-Womenomics Workplace Victory

You give yourself a confidence-boosting pep talk that runs something like this: I've already done everything that I needed to do, and more. I've come through on a project when the odds were against me. I'm not adding any value to the company sitting here. Anything extra can be handled by e-mail later. I not only can go home, but I should go home.

If you'd had a real handle on your mental game, you wouldn't have even hesitated to go home in the first place. You would have known that the confidence—in yourself and in your work— that you would show by approaching your boss, giving a quick rundown of where everything stands, and saying good-bye would outshine almost every other consideration. You don't want your boss to think you're not a hard worker, but think about it, you spent plenty of time already proving you are one. By going home, resting, spending some time with your family, and relaxing, you'll be able to come back tomorrow and show your boss the same thing again.

The outlasting-the-boss game is just one example of what happens when our priorities get muddied by our perception of someone else's priorities. But escaping that trap takes a major mental adjustment that involves *really* knowing what you want from life and work. It's about defining your goals, and pruning other people's. For well-educated, ambitious, committed women this mental process can be harder than anything else we're going to ask you to do in this book. But once you have it, you will have slain the ego dragon and be on your way to a saner, more integrated, more satisfying existence. Ready?

Let's start with that age-old question:

What do you really want from life?

Warning! Do not put down this book and mutter disapprovingly about the uselessness of New Age psychobabble. We get very practical very fast. Trust us.

When you are seventy years old, looking back at your many productive years, what will make you feel good about the life you've led? What do you need to do now to maximize satisfaction and minimize regrets?

OK—are you starting to see our thinking?

Chances are that if you've picked up this book, your feelings about work are complicated, just as they are for hundreds of well-educated women we know. You saw those numbers in chapter 2. You, like most of us, want a job that satisfies you intellectually but leaves you enough time to lead a fulfilling personal life as well. That's your long-buried need. And it should be your clear definition of success. But the truth is that for most of us it's not that easy. We rebel against it because it's not the "traditional" way of doing things.

But have you ever stopped to wonder why most of us are so inherently uncomfortable with the "work till you drop to make it to the top" model? Even as we feel we should be pursuing it? Let us suggest the following: we are uncomfortable with it because it doesn't fit who we are. It never has. Because it's not success as defined *by women, for women*. It's somebody else's version of a successful life. Somebody of a different gender. It's not what we want.

Don't panic. If a less hierarchical concept of success sounds appealing to you, it doesn't mean you aren't ambitious, smart, professional, or committed. Far from it. You want to remain engaged in your professional life. You don't really want to sit in a playroom and sing nursery rhymes all day, but you *do* want more time for your life. It is nothing to be ashamed of.

Saying I want some life with my work—or even, I want some work with my life—is not renouncing your ideals; it's understanding, accepting, and embracing your fundamental desires.

And don't be hard on yourself if you're already finding this exercise in honesty exhausting and troubling. Don't stop now, even if you feel that such thoughts are heretical, maybe even disloyal. We know, because we've been through it, that it is surprisingly hard to turn down the noise of social and professional expectations and tune in to a clear, confident, and personal definition of success.

We have a list of questions we've put together over the years that has helped us find our right track. It's a list we still run through every time we face a career change or feel we're off course or risk going off course. If someone offers us a new job, or our boss asks us to take on a new challenge, we go back to this list. It's our "Womenomics gut check."

So here we go. You may need to put aside a quiet afternoon to think about this, or mull it over for a few days or even weeks. And remember, it only works if you answer with absolute honesty.

----

womenomics
Gut Check

PROFESSIONAL ACHIEVEMENT

1. How important is your career to you?

2. The above is hard to answer in isolation, right? So think about how important your career is compared to other aspects of your life. Make a pie chart, a numbered list, a graph—whatever works—and see how it rates compared to family, hobbies, or other interests. Now you can see how important your career is in relation to the other things in your life.

3. When you think about your work, what is it you enjoy most about it? The work itself, your status, the sense of power you have, the getting out of the house, the gossiping with coworkers, the money? Take a stab at ranking this list.

4. How much of the way you work is about satisfying your ego? How much of it is about a sense of competition? Do you feel driven to do it the same as, or better than, everyone else?

5. Are you prepared to give up money to get more time? And can you afford it? If you think creatively, then you'll often see you might be able to make do with a bit less.

FAMILY/LIFE

1. Do you spend enough time with your children/aged parent/community group/sport? What is enough time? For you—not anyone else?

2. What brings you the most joy, fulfillment, excitement in your life? Make that list.

3. Would having more time to devote to family or yourself make a difference in your life? Be realistic. Don't fantasize about long, lazy days at home with your kids playing happily outside as you roll homemade pasta. Think about what you'd actually do with another few hours each day or week. Would you be able to pick the kids up from school? Coach a soccer team? Take your father to the park? How meaningful would that extra time be? How do you feel when you imagine it?

STRESS

1. What regularly brings the most stress into your life? Where does work rate? Get specific. What situations at work or at home are the most tense? (Again, lay it out with lists or charts or graphs. Sometimes actually putting it on paper clarifies the thought process. We like pros and cons lists; try those out too.)

2. If you have significant stress at or over work, is it about time? What might help? Working fewer hours? Having a more flexible schedule? Or would it require a new boss or a new career? Really be a sleuth here and uncover what you like least.

3. Picture the next move up on the ladder, or the promotion you've been eyeing. Do you get a total rush? Is the adrenaline tinged with anxiety? Do you even have a sense of dread about how you might manage it?

NIRVANA

1. Pretend for a moment that you are totally in charge of dictating the structure of your daily life. If you could create the ideal situation, the perfect mix of work and personal life, what would it be?

2. Now get specific. How many hours a week would you like to work? Fifteen? Thirty-five? Fifty-five? And what would the schedule look like? Be creative.

3. Next, imagine yourself in another situation. You've said no to the promotion, or you've asked to work less. What do you feel? Anxious? A failure? Lazy? Strip away all of the negativity. Do you also feel a secret sense of relief?

Once you've wrestled with these questions as honestly and clearly as you can, you should have made a pretty good start at unearthing your core preferences. You may, in fact, see the pattern. Success, for most of us, is not necessarily earning top dollar or amassing top status; it's a complex, nuanced web of personal and professional goals. Finally coming to terms with that can feel like the moment when Dorothy lands in Oz—shades of gray dissolve to reveal a vibrant world of possibility. We can define our own success. And *that*—let us tell you—is real power.

You may well find that the answers to these questions change at different stages of your life, but the point of the exercise doesn't. These gut-check questions will provide you with a definition of what you want and, just as importantly, will keep you on the right track. Every time you make a professional decision, run through the survey. See how the job or career change you are contemplating stacks up against your answers. Does it fit them? If not it probably isn't the right move for you. It may be, later on, but not now. And go back to these questions whenever you feel anxious about keeping your life sane. You will find they act as a reassuring guide.

Of course simply knowing what we really want doesn't get us to the finish line. Many women may understand they are not working according to their own true goals, but they still don't take action—because that would mean pushing through a thicket of ego, financial, and even feminist barricades. But keep reading. You'll see that most of these walls will topple with just a tap.

Face Your Fears

Linda Brooks is a true pioneer. She's a super-brainiac, an honors graduate of an elite law school, and a partner at a top New York law firm. But she's a new kind of partner—an "80 percent" partner. After years of slogging through her work-to-the-max schedule, Linda now has every Friday off. It might not sound so radical, but in the hard-driven New York legal profession, hers is a remarkable situation. And her demand for change had nothing to do with children or family.

"I was in my early thirties and had no marriage, no boyfriend because I was married to my job; I didn't even have a plant that's alive. And so you start going to therapy and they're telling you,

'You're identifying too much with your work' and you kind of see the problem, but you just can't escape it. So I start slowly thinking, 'Well, I don't see anything changing here. I don't see anything getting any better if I don't make a big change.'"

Linda (we had to change her name because her arrangement is so unusual that she's still worried about rocking the boat) is thrilled now with her Fridays-off change, one that she says is giving her time for yoga, dancing lessons, and to work on a book.

But by far the most difficult part of the process was taming her fear that reduced hours would inevitably mean reduced status. "The things *we* tell *ourselves*—it's like compounding the negative talk when you're trying to work less. It's an amplifier. Every single little mistake you make, you say 'Oh my God! My career is over! What have I done, this is the most ridiculous thing, I'm going to lose all my clients. If I were a client, why would I ever pick someone that may be out on a Friday when I need them.'"

You, like Linda, have probably come to the realization that something needs to change. The next psychological step is to understand that a change in status won't spike your career. In fact, it may not affect it much at all.

"I really enjoy my job now when I'm doing it, but it's not everything anymore. I just have other aspects of my personality that are starting to develop. I'm learning what I like to do!" she exclaims.

Maria Souder has always been competitive, with her schoolmates, her friends, even herself. She flew through Georgia Tech with honors. And she was always planning. "After five years I'll do this, and after two more years I'll do this. I had always been structured at school. I wanted to graduate with high honors or I wanted to be a part of this organization and I wanted to be successful in this and be known on campus for that." She smiles.

Maria became an engineer and got her MBA while working at Georgia Power. One of the few women climbing up the ladder in a male-dominated field, she relished the pace, the crises, the twelve-hour days, until she had baby Xavier. "I actually started to break out in spots," she remembers, "just dealing with the stress I was putting on myself to succeed and do everything to perfection." The thirty-two-year-old decided a few years ago to make a dramatic change. She'd give up her almost certain shot at becoming plant manager and move into environmental affairs—still challenging, but off the main macho track of power generation.

"I was very scared, because I was stepping out from a structure that I knew," she explains. "You have expertise and achievement and then all of a sudden you put the brakes on and change directions. And I think that probably was a shock—maybe to some other people as well."

Yes, it can be frightening. And again, we are hard-core realists. You *will* give something up. Eventually it won't seem like a sacrifice, and it won't seem like the psychic earthquake Maria describes, but it will take some time to get to that point. One of the greatest challenges is simply overcoming your own demons about what scaling back might mean. Almost all of our Womenomics women have put themselves through some sort of drill to help face down their fears. Ours is called the Womenomics "what if" exercise. The point? Not necessarily to uncover clear answers to our "what ifs" but rather to embrace that long-held psychological view that simply confronting fears takes away most of the scare.

Pour yourself a drink. This exercise is tough—a grisly, grown-up version of a haunted house ride. We're going to zip through all of those bone-chilling, worst-case scenario consequences that pop up in the dark corners of your mind when you consider kicking down the ladder. With the lights on, you'll usually see your fears are nothing more than dime-store skele-tons with good sound effects.

Strap in, and let's get started.

- -

womenomics
What-if Exercise

- Imagine the face your boss will make if you take yourself out of the running for that big job. Will he look at you like you are speaking Swahili, as he wonders to himself why he ever invested in you?

- You tell your supervisor you want to cut your time at the office. Will he shake his head and say in that annoyingly paternal baritone that you have such promise and he's disappointed in your choice, as you awkwardly twist your hands?

- As you walk by the office watercooler will you hear mutterings of "lost her ambition" floating in your wake?

- Will you get only the most boring, meaningless assignments from now on?

- Will you lose your window office, your swagger, your drive?

- Will you stare blankly at people at cocktail parties who badger you about what you are planning for your next career move?

- Will you go broke?

- Will they say no?

- Will you be fired?

- -

You get the picture. Put your own spin on this line of questioning and interrogate yourself until you reach Geneva Convention Limits or you run out of alcohol. And no, this isn't gratuitous torture. By working through exactly what might happen, or rather what you fear might happen, you will come to see the very worst is not at all likely. And that is a critical realization. If you don't confront the fears that lurk in your head and ruthlessly unmask them, these nebulous dark feelings can balloon completely out of proportion and paralyze you. Irrational fear may be the worst enemy of Womenomics.

By doing this exercise you'll have a better grasp of what might actually happen, and be prepared for it. But you'll likely see that the consequences aren't such a big deal.

Oh, sure, your boss might not immediately give you the ideal schedule (not to mention absolute freedom). We've both faced considerable detours on our journeys. And what we've found is that the very worst thing that can happen when you ask for more time is that they say no. No broken bones, no firings. All the rest can be handled. But a practice run-through of the gauntlet of judgment you might face is essential survival training.

Bottom line: once you really feel comfortable with what you want, these "worst-case scenarios" actually don't bother you so much. You tune out the raised eyebrows and the hallway commentary. And then, guess what, something else happens: people get back to their own career concerns and the gossip about you stops.

Even a super high achiever like eBay's former CEO, Meg Whitman, has gone through the process of bucking the corporate culture and setting her own parameters. Whitman was working as a young, ambitious management consultant at Bain & Company when she had her first child. (She didn't even dare tell her boss until she was seven months pregnant—you see, times are changing!) After her son was born she made an executive decision that was almost unheard of in that high-octane business world: she would leave every day at a reasonable hour. "I said, short of crisis, I am going to actually walk out of here at five-thirty," she told us. "I did not want to hang around as so many of the guys were." Still, she was concerned. "It was very social, it was very young, not too many of the guys had kids and I was worried about that."

But Whitman found an unexpected psychological benefit to her new baby-enforced hours—she felt liberated. "In my mind I had a little excuse for not making partner. I sort of said, 'OK if I don't make partner it is because I have made this family trade-off.' And it had a really interesting effect. I got 20 percent more efficient and actually gained confidence because I had let myself off the hook in a funny way."

Solving the Status Trap

There is one little hitch in this process of redefining success on our own terms. Or for some of us, one stubborn, out-size hitch. Our egos. Even if you feel the satisfaction and clarity of knowing what you really want, and you understand it won't mean the end of your professional life, your ego, well nurtured as a successful professional woman, will keep popping up to undermine your evolution.

Ego can, of course, be a powerful and positive force in life. But the status trap forms when we start to measure ourselves by standards not truly our own. Evaluating your life by someone else's goals provides just enough drive to keep going—to seek the next promotion, the bigger bonus, the nicer car, or the better job title—but it doesn't provide enough satisfaction to make you happy. You've probably experienced the feeling of getting a raise, a promotion, or a nice bonus, and instead of being elated, as you expected, you feel a bit let down. The shiny new thing that you earned seems, in hindsight, more like bait than a reward. And what you now face is more hours, more meetings, more stress— and less of what you truly enjoy.

The status trap is like a pool of professional quicksand that, the farther into it you get, the more it pulls. The force that sucks you in is a mental one that springs from your sense of responsibility, your desire to do "more and better," your personal connections at work, and, simply, your misguided ego. Getting out of the professional quicksand requires that you first become aware that you're in it. And then you can employ a set of concrete defenses that will let you defeat the status trap altogether.

When we first met her, Christine Heenan was being asked to interview for a top job running Harvard University's communications and public affairs departments. Christine had spent the last seven years running her own communications company in Rhode Island. She was also teaching at Brown, where she used to be a senior administrator, and before that had worked in the Clinton White House. Up in Rhode Island, she had been feeling left out of that alpha loop.

"I remember being at a wedding in Quebec with former colleagues from the White House. There were lots of women my age I reconnected with at this wedding who were doing fascinating things. There was one who'd just finished law school and was now working on human trafficking issues. There was another who was head of communications for NBC and did all sorts of incredible things, and I sort of felt, 'Oh, let me tell you about my boys Alex and Colin.' Don't get me wrong, I am so proud of my kids and proud of what I've done professionally with my company, but without question, in my field, there is just this professional corridor from New York to D.C. that I was outside of."

So when that interest came from Harvard, Christine was flattered. It was an ego-boosting call from her previous top-tier life. It was also, ego aside, a very appealing job. But Christine had spent years in Rhode Island building a career that gave her a perfect fit between her office life and her home life; she had made workplace flexibility a real cornerstone of her company, and she was very reluctant to give up that freedom. The Harvard job would mean working for someone else again, with someone else's hours. It would mean good-bye to control, and hello to corporate restraints. She was torn.

"One of my reactions was relief." She says, "I'm glad I'm still thought of for a job like that. I'm glad I haven't taken myself out of sight for those kinds of professional opportunities."

But as Christine looked her ego solidly in the eye, she realized she didn't *need* the Harvard job. She told the recruiters it was a dream job for her, but a dream that would be best to pursue once her children were older.

Sarah Slusser is a divorced and remarried forty-five-year-old mother of two boys and a senior vice president at AES, an energy company in Virginia, where she puts together deals to build power plants all over the world. She is smart, effective, and would be a big catch for any high-powered financial firm. Sarah works in a world of multimillion-dollar business transactions. She is very good at what she does and could make significantly more than her current salary if she switched to any number of financial firms. She should know, because she's in the habit of having to turn down well-paying job offers—and every time she does, she finds it's hard on her ego.

"The ego issue, it's very difficult," Sarah acknowledges. "When I'm having lunch with friends, it's fine. It's when I'm at work that it's harder to reconcile. I used to lead a team, but I scaled back, and now I don't. You sit in these meetings with people who are executive vice presidents and you know you could do the job just as well but you've chosen not to, in order to have time for the kids. It is hard."

Sarah has a tip for reconciling her professional ambition and shaken ego with her decision not to take those promotions. "I deal with it by frequently reminding myself of why I've made these choices—of all the reasons for not being at the position I was before. I keep telling myself it's worth it, so that I can pick my son up from school or whatever. But I do have to remind myself."

The very fact that our energy star entertains these offers is testament to her ambition. And maybe the offers themselves, even if they're not accepted, serve as a useful psychological boost. "I think that's why I like getting these job offers," Sarah says. "Maybe it's part of why I entertain them. It feels good to be wanted. I've just been appointed director of the board of a New York hedge fund I worked with—when they sent me the press release, it felt good. I hadn't realized they were going to send out a press release. And it was nice."

But Sarah is clear: while her two boys are still young, she won't move, even for a job that recently offered her multiples of her current salary.

"You earn flexibility by staying at one organization and rising up and that then becomes really hard to trade in. Really hard," she says. "Anyway, you only need so much money, right?"

The important part of this mind adjustment is not just knowing what you want and what you don't want, but it is also living that realization day to day.

KATTY   Ego is a big, big problem in television. Our careers feed off being seen. The more recognized we are, the more well-known we become, the more our organizations value us and the more they pay us. It is a seductive and very slippery slope. Because once you've tasted a little fame, you tend to want more, and as with all addictive confections, there can never be enough. Soon you are trading far too much to get your pixilated features on a TV screen. As my television career began to expand I discovered the pitfalls of this status seduction. People began to recognize me. Not Katie Couric recognize of course, but just occasionally someone in the local Safeway or someone in the airport check-in line would say, "Hey, don't I know you from somewhere?" or, even, "Wow, I'm such a fan. I just love your British accent/pink jacket/new hairdo, or (rarely) your views on politics." I have to admit, though I'm embarrassed to do so, I liked it. It made me feel somehow important, and I stupidly started to fall for the dumb idea that if more people recognized me, I wouldn't just feel more important I would actually be more important. This made me susceptible to job offers that clearly fell way outside my personal goal posts. Sure, I'd muse, I can work sixty-hour weeks, fifty-two weeks a year, be on call round the clock if it just gets me more of those pixels and the prospect of my face on the back of that bus. Believe me, I understand the draw of ego. And even now, when I'm offered more airtime or more blog time I still have to deal with the internal battle between the demon voice of my ego and the sensible voice of my life-balance. I can still be seduced by the flattery of my boss saying how great it is that his boss wants more of me on air. And I still have to go back to our gut check and assess whether this new offer really suits my life. Fortunately the voice of life-balance usually wins over the voice of ego and ends up shouting, "Are you CRAZY? You have too much on your plate already, just get a grip!" I try to listen to that voice.

The Ego Reboot

Whenever you have one of those inevitable ego moments, thinking to yourself what you could have achieved, how much you might be earning, whose former office and job title you could be brandishing, you should stop yourself and hit the ego REBOOT button.

Ego is a natural and healthy thing, but to make sure the influence of your ego stays positive, you need to focus it correctly. This is what the Ego Reboot is all about.

The process of getting back on track begins with pausing to recognize that you're starting to fall down the rabbit hole of an egotistical fantasy— otherwise known as an ego trip.

Then think honestly about the day-to-day nitty-gritty that you would have to endure to even have a shot of achieving whatever accolade or position your ego is driving you to think about. Think about the hours, the bosses, the meetings, the exhaustion, and all the other things we already know too well.

Finally, visualize one (or more) of the positive, tangible things that taking a different approach to your life makes possible. It might be a morning run, dinner with your kids, or simply having time to read a book. The trick is to actually picture these things in your mind.

So, the three steps of the Ego Reboot:

1. Pause and Recognize that you're going on an ego trip.

2. Realize the Day-to-Day Reality of what you're fantasizing about.

3. Visualize the Positives of newfound free time and a more balanced life.

As with anything else, if you practice this three-step process a few times it will start to become natural, and in time, your ego's yearning for the things it previously valued will be transformed into a feeling of satisfaction with the new positives that you've earned.

Confronting the Feminist Ideal

Here's another and rather unexpected piece in the mental challenge—how to handle our debt to our pioneering feminist forebears. It's a complicated relationship—part gratitude, part admiration, part guilt, part rejection. We know that women thirty years ago fought hard to get all of us a seat at the table. They fought so hard that they couldn't let up. They built a model of women as equal to men, pulling sixty-hour weeks without a murmur of complaint. They've brought women to the forefront of fields as diverse as business, academics, politics, and journalism. We are all in their debt for taking those early difficult steps and demanding the right and opportunity to take them.

But that doesn't mean that the way they worked, and had to work, is right for most of us now. The work pace that enabled them to break down those boardroom doors was necessary at the time, but today we have other choices. We both still think of ourselves as feminists, but it's a new brand of feminism we adhere to. It is a feminism that finally allows us to build our own work-life model, one that permits us to be who we really want to be.

So here's your challenge. As you attempt to make positive changes in your life, you may encounter skepticism or criticism from some of your elders, those who've been in the trenches.

Or you may simply feel such an immense sense of understandable loyalty to these women that you don't want to "let them down." Or you may feel committed to the "we must be exactly equal" school of feminist thinking, and you may struggle with what seems to be inequality.

When you find yourself in the middle of this feminist tangle, real or imagined, remember the following:

- Plenty of new research, as you saw in chapter 2, supports the conclusion that women are wired to enjoy a different version of success.

- Women are now in a position where we are able not only to participate in the working world but also to influence it and change it. What could possibly be more empowering as a woman than not just to sit at the table but also to change the way it looks, based on our own perspectives as women? Isn't that a feminist breakthrough as well?

- Finally, it is natural to focus on the women before us—the ones who paved the way, and who are often our bosses! But you need to think about another group just as important: the young women who come after us. Having the boldness to choose a life that you want for yourself is not a selfish move. In fact, like the feminists before us, confronting and surmounting our new challenges as women gives the next generation of women another level of choices and another layer of freedom so that they can live exactly the kind of life they want to live.

Turning Costs into Benefits

By now, you've realized that there are enormous benefits to re-shaping your life to suit your real wants and needs. Of course, where there's a benefit there's also a cost. Quantifying these costs and benefits is a difficult and highly personal task. While we can't crunch the individual numbers for you, we can definitely help you look at the problem through the right lens. And that is critical, because the heart of Womenomics is really about seeing the world in a new way.

For starters, the notion of what a cost or a benefit is depends on your values. If you're on a nonstop money hunt, then a 10 percent raise is a definite benefit, even if the cost is more hours of work every week.

If, however, you're seeking a well-rounded life that embraces your family, your passions, and the simple joy of a small amount of free time each week, then things begin to look different.

It's this difference that's most important when you think of cost-benefit analysis, Womenomics style. What we've been trying to show you in this chapter is that the mental game is about getting past some of the most serious obstacles—the internal, personal ones—and finding real success. Now, we want you to start putting the ideas of the mental game into practice.

Time Versus Money

According to the traditional way of thinking, losing time as you earn more money isn't seen as a cost at all. But looking through a Womenomics lens, additional time is increasingly more valuable than more money. Indeed, time is the currency of Womenomics.

It's remarkable how much money most professional women would be prepared to give up to earn themselves a few more free hours every week. It's a bit like high-stakes financial trading, where we sell short on one commodity to hold another that's even more valuable.

But it is worth reminding ourselves that we are the lucky ones. We are in the very fortunate position of being able to choose to give up some income in order to earn some time. If you are poor in New York or New Delhi, you don't have that option. This choice is a luxury, and we as professional women should appreciate how incredibly fortunate we are.

How much time you need and how much money you will forfeit to get that time are questions only you can answer. Everyone's definition of what it means to have enough time is different.

Similarly, everyone's definition of what it means to have enough money is different. You'll need to look honestly at that side of the equation too. If you are miserable without a regular splurge at your favorite clothing store, if life without foreign travel seems unbearable, or if you need every penny for your son's violin lessons, you may have to compromise on your time or simply work on the efficiency side of the equation. (We'll tell you later in the book how to save time without making major career changes.)

When Jennifer Dickey chose to trade money for time, it was worth it, but it wasn't easy. The thirty-one-year-old is a mechanical engineer at the architectural firm Kahn Associates in Detroit. On Jennifer's floor of a hundred employees there are only seven women in total. She is a woman in a man's world who has struggled with the financial costs of dialing back her work hours.

Jennifer has two young daughters. After her second child was born, she realized she didn't want to work a forty-hour week anymore. Her firm was known for allowing employees to work flexibly, so there was no problem getting the agreement. The problem came in financing it. Jennifer could take the pay cut in her hourly salary without too much hardship. Her husband works in sales, so they had a second income.

What she hadn't factored in was that all her company benefits would be cut proportionately as well. For every hour she wanted to take off from her traditional forty-hour week, Jennifer would pay a benefits price. Her company's Social Security contributions would go down. She would get less paid vacation. Meanwhile she would have to pay out more for her share of the company's health insurance program.

"You know I can handle losing a few hours a week of salary, but it's all of the costs that go along with it that are also prorated, and that adds up," she says.

At the same time that Jennifer was working out this time/ money equation, her eldest daughter turned three, and they enrolled her in preschool. That cost was $100 per week, and because they had family living nearby who'd looked after the girls until then, it was the first time Jennifer had paid for child care. The preschool payouts and salary cut came as a double whammy.

"My second daughter was born in December, I came back to work in March, and I don't think I made the decision to cut hours until it was the end of the summer because I was very nervous about it," says Jennifer. "I was nervous about making the move because it was a big financial difference for us."

For Jennifer those "hidden" costs meant she could only cut her hours from forty to thirty-six. It seems small, but even those extra four hours have helped. If she and her husband can make it work financially she would like to cut back to a thirty-hour week. Her ideal would be to work three ten-hour days.

For Jennifer, this was a fairly straightforward value trade. But it takes practice to see this, to get to the point where a financial sacrifice is "worth it."

----

the womenomics
Balance Sheet

To help you get your head in the game, we've made a list of some of the other important "costs" we all worry about as we try to get to the New All. What will quickly become clear, we hope, is that what initially appears a cost might not be costly at all and may yield significant "hidden benefits."

COST 1 } *"Isn't a pay cut of any sort a big step backward?"*

HIDDEN BENEFIT 1

Don't think hourly rate— think value, as Jennifer discovered. Even if you have to make financial cutbacks, the value to your life of gaining a few extra hours each week is potentially huge. It can make the difference between sanity and chaos.

And remember: every minute is not created equal. If you can be home between four and six to pick up the kids, or have a Friday afternoon to go for your beloved run, or a regular day to meet with a group of friends, it can add a level of satisfaction to your life that money literally cannot buy. So before you brand taking a pay cut as an indulgence, let your imagination explore the idea of taking that pay cut so you can have a few hours to do all the small but intensely meaningful things that seemed unachievable from the perspective of your office desk.

KATTY   If only I did have a dollar for every time I am asked "How do you do it?" I really would be a moderately wealthy woman. But that might be my only chance at big wealth because the truth is I don't work that hard, not if your measure is hours.

I have a mental clock running in my head. If it ticks over thirty hours a week, I am doing too much and need to cut something out. My ideal workweek has me away from home no more than twenty-five hours. Of course, there are times when I have to put in a lot more—try an election year to test your short work week resolve! But then I make sure I take time off afterward. My first question for any new project: how much time will it take? My first thought about any new job: can I do it and still have time? If not, I know it's not worth it. I have turned down better paying jobs to keep control of my hours. The afternoons I have free to surprise my eight-year-old with a school pickup or the (relatively) quiet Monday mornings with my youngest planting herbs in the yard—nobody could buy those back from me, at any price.

COST 2 } *"But money, and the symbolic power of money, defines who I am."*

HIDDEN BENEFIT 2

It doesn't actually, and it certainly shouldn't. Taking your ego out of your income is a surprisingly liberating move. If you are trading money for time, in addition to literally gaining more hours to raise responsible children or contribute in other ways to society or a saner life, you also remove a false mental measuring stick that saps positive energy. When you measure yourself on something as flimsy as salary, it drains your ability to feel satisfied with your actual work or other accomplishments.

COST 3 } *"I don't want to confront my boss about this. She'll think I'm lazy and unmotivated and she'll stop assigning me the best projects."*

HIDDEN BENEFIT 3

Confronting your boss can actually make you look good.

You'll find that having the courage and confidence to define what you will and won't do shows strength. Bosses admire people who have limits and who are willing to defend themselves. In fact, rather than showing that you're unmotivated, explaining what you want and need shows that you are active and ready to think outside the box in order to create change.

Believe us, it may seem impossible, but it's truly a "positive" in disguise. And if you do good work, nobody thinks you're lazy these days. We'll tell you more about these negotiations in chapter 6.

COST 4 } *"My coworkers may not like it and may think less of me."*

HIDDEN BENEFIT 4

Maybe . . . but do you really care? Does it really matter? In general, people think what they're going to think, since their reactions are their own choice and responsibility. In reality, however, your coworkers will probably be envious of what you managed to pull off. And those who don't simply forget about it after a few weeks will probably approach you to gain pointers. Indeed, some will likely start to see you as a role model or mentor and may be emboldened to take a similar path.

COST 5 } *"It's not fair. I'm sacrificing and my husband isn't. Why do I have to give up more than he does?"*

HIDDEN BENEFIT 5

Remember, time does not have the same value for everybody. And especially at home, this is not a zero sum game.

An extra hour a day of time with our children may be worth ten times to us what it is to somebody else—even our spouses. Part of our confidence to fight for time to be home more came from understanding that *we're* the ones who want to be with our children. It's sometimes easy in those frantic, two-working-parent households to slip into the "Well, if you only came home earlier I wouldn't need to" argument. We know. We've both done it—given our husbands a hard time for not being home enough. But this is really about *our* time with our kids. We're the lucky ones to get that extra time with them.

(By the way, just as you don't want to be judged on how much time you need, you will find this work/life math a whole lot easier if you don't try to judge other people's time or priorities either. As we were researching this book we came across the story of a man who went to his boss to ask for shorter hours at work. "Well," said the boss, "we can probably work something out, but what do you want it for?" "To spend more time with my dog," the man replied! Who are we to say that this choice isn't valuable.)

Success Redefined

As you've seen, winning the mental game is key to overcoming the obstacles to the New All. We face a whole array of challenges in this area, from basic considerations, like earning enough money, to worrying about how we'll be perceived by people around us for taking a different approach to work and life, to even feeling a sense of guilt for "giving up" what so many hardworking women struggled to have the opportunity to achieve.

The important thing to remember is that, first, all these fears and worries are natural. After all, how significant could a life change be if it wasn't accompanied by some worries and fears?

The second thing to remember is that each of these fears or worries has a real-life, workable solution. You don't need to climb Everest or check in to a Buddhist monastery to gain this new perspective. You only need to acknowledge the fears, confront them, and, most importantly, stay focused on your real desires and goals.

You are well on you way now. You have readjusted your definition of success and decided you don't need to put in those long hours to prove your worth. You can give yourself permission to jump off the ladder, carve your own path, and have a better life. There's just one more thing you need to do: change your mind-set so that you are *proud* of not being tied to the office for hours.

This is success—you shouldn't feel sheepish about it. Rather, shout it from the rooftops that you want to have an interesting job, time for your family, *and* a life.

We know that the chances of your boss actually congratulating you on your new attitude as you leave the office at 3 P.M., or better still, when you don't come in at all, are pretty minimal. But how about giving yourself a pat on the back? How about going a step further by rejecting the myth that you can only be proud of logging megalong hours? How about turning the whole work/time/success equation upside down and thinking that if you can have an interesting job and not kill yourself in the process—that is a REAL success story?

Maria Souder of Georgia Power has come to realize just that. Remember how terrified she felt about the change she was about to make? Well, her bosses actually reacted very well to her career switch and have made it clear she can move back over to the power-generation side of the business at any time. Many days now, Maria has the time to watch her son for a while in his class before she picks him up. She chats with his teacher and then takes him swimming. She's thrilled with her new position and her new time. "I brought things back into perspective, back into balance, and I just think it's amazing," she says, shaking her head. "I look back and I just can't figure out why this revelation didn't come sooner, as to how we should live our lives and how we should balance things."

We've both spent years pretending more time at work is our life's ambition. We, like many women we know, have even succumbed to boasting about how late we have to work—as if that's really some kind of achievement. We've nodded earnestly when colleagues talked about how they couldn't possibly take more than two weeks vacation a year.

Why do we buy into that outdated, macho construct of hours on the job being the definition of success?

Well, mostly because it makes us feel SOOO important. If we have to work round the clock it somehow gives the impression that our companies really depend on us, so much so that they couldn't possibly survive if we headed home at 5 P.M. or disappeared on vacation. Oh no, we are indispensable! We can't be away: the corporate edifice would crumble!

Companies increasingly realize that what's important is what you produce, not how, where, and when you do it. The measure of success in this new business environment is changing.

We think that if you can set a professional goal, achieve it, and have time left over, then you really are a superstar. Let's face it, many of us could easily run the world if we spent fifteen hours a day at our desk. Most competent, professional women could—and some do. But isn't it just as impressive, perhaps even more so, to have achieved a new, freer, more integrated all? That's our new balance sheet, and we believe it is the real definition of a successful woman.

news you can use

1. Define what YOU really want—not what others say you should want.

2. Sidestep the status trap—it's a false ego rush.

3. Face your fears and do the math: the costs of making changes turn quickly into benefits when you use a Womenomics eyeshade.

good-bye guilt (and hello no)

Women have been bearing the burden of guilt since the beginning of history. Adam takes a bite of the fateful apple and—oh sure, blame it on Eve. The original guilt. And unfortunately, we women make it easy. We silently put "getting kicked out of paradise" on a long list of things to feel guilty about over the ages.

Guilt is such a daunting problem for women as they try to change the way they work that we feel it demands a chapter all its own. But this is a good news chapter. We'll help you see how one insidious emotion can prevent you from getting the professional life you really want. Guilt can stop you from leaving the office at 3 P.M. to make the school pickup, even though you've finished your workday's tasks. It can keep you from turning down those extra assignments your male colleagues just don't want to do. It can scuttle a day off, even though you're owed it.

Look—we have a natural gift for emotions of all sorts, and as we pointed out in chapter 1, that can work in our favor. But unleash too much of a good thing, too much intuition and empathy, and suddenly you've fallen into a pitched battle with that destructive menace, guilt, and its evil stepsister, the need to please. Here we'll hand you a map to guide you around all of these guilt-ridden pitfalls so that you can actually reach your New All.

Believe it or not, there are women out there who have harnessed their emotions and put them to use working *for* their benefit, instead of *against* it. You'll see in this chapter that you don't have to adopt a program of incense-filled meditation (though again, if that's your thing, by all means . . .), but that you can take concrete, realistic steps to banish this cunning, negative emotion, and at the same time, keep the positive, quintessentially female ones that make you who you are.

Like all things, it takes practice and dedication. Fortunately, if you're a professional woman, you're probably very good at those two things. In this chapter we'll take a hard look at your emotional bad habits, give you a process that will get the principal culprit, guilt, out of your life, and then teach you the empowering positivity of the word *no* and how to wield it. The ability to use that critical little word, *no*, is the ultimate sign that you have your guilt-infused emotions in check. It means you can really start to ask for what you want.

Linda Brooks, our part-time partner at that tony New York law firm, says the biggest challenge to what she achieved was almost certainly emotional. And she counsels associates who want to follow in her footsteps that they have to be ready to withstand emotional riptides.

"I do think that person is going to need a little bit more confidence than the associate standing next to her," she says. "You know, it takes balls to stand up halfway to partnership and say 'I want a life!' And to say 'I want a life, and I'm going to be a partner and try to do both things.' I think that's wonderful, but I do think it takes a little more confidence, to not get paranoid and feel guilty and throw up your hands when things start to get tough."

Guilt: The Useless Emotion

Think of it this way—we now know that our brain structure and chemistry make us more evolved, more able to anticipate consequences, and more ready to empathize with others than men are. The proverbial sixth sense is a woman's sense—it's the ability to tune in to and understand unspoken things that men don't even know exist.

But the downside is our guilt. It's really the flip side of all of that good stuff. Because we are so empathetic and connected, we're also hyperaware of what could be or should be or what might have been or should have been or who could be feeling what and—of course—why it's all our fault.

Claire's typical 5 minute all-consuming stream of consciousness, self-blame soundtrack— aka the guilt trip:

Even as I write this sentence, I feel bad leaving Della with our wonderful nanny, whom she loves dearly. Though I'm off work today, I really should be thinking about that upcoming report on the anniversary of Bobby Kennedy's assassination—otherwise it might not be artful enough. I have friends coming for dinner and I'm going to have to buy prepared food. Will they be disappointed? I still haven't called those nice people back from that medical report I did to be sure they were happy with it. Could they be mad? Our house is a wreck, I have ants in my office, my kids will clearly be marred by all of the chaos and disorganization around here. I still haven't shopped for my husband's birthday. Are the people putting in carpet downstairs OK? They seem hungry. Should I go buy them sandwiches?

Amazon.com can provide you with hundreds of guilt-banishing tomes to help with these issues. And it takes a tome (at the very least) to excise guilt completely from your mentality. Right now, we're only taking on a narrow, but critical, slice of the jumbo-size American woman's guilt pie: you must learn to keep that useless emotion from standing in the way of your goals—from forcing you to say yes to more work than you want. You need to feel good, not guilty, about getting what you want from your career. In fact, guilt is more self-indulgent than self-correcting, since it alone doesn't actually help you, your coworkers, your kids, or your boss.

This is an area where you are negotiating with yourself not your boss. But if you do it properly we guarantee it will save you huge amounts of time at work.

The key, then, is to be aware that guilt, when you haven't actually done anything wrong, is a useless emotion. Keep repeating it to yourself: just junk guilt. Just junk guilt.

Guilt Trips: The Classics

If you're not sure whether or not guilt has a stranglehold on your work life (or any other part of your life), check out our most popular guilt trips. Sound familiar? Most of you will see that you have some work to do.

> *—You're sitting in the park with the kids on your assigned day off, the sun is shining on your back, nobody's fighting (yeah right—but you get the drift), and in the back of your*

mind, you're worried about the sudden work crunch in the office. Shouldn't you be there helping out, rather than playing here in the park? Are you a bad person because you are not working?

Or

—You've finished your assignments and you decide to leave the office. You're not needed, you've added your value for the day, you've made it clear to your boss early on that you don't stay in the office if you're not actually needed. Still, it is only lunchtime. As you head for your coat, you are painfully aware of all of your colleagues sitting diligently at their desks. There it is again—guilt setting in. You should stay at the office, right?

Or

—You say "no" to extra work generally because it's not part of your brief, and frankly you'd rather spend that time at home. But still, whenever you're asked and you have to say "no," yet again, the guilt descends. Maybe if you just said "yes" this one time, that would make up for all of the others?

Or

—You have an extra week's vacation to use up before the end of the year but your colleagues don't seem to have taken even half of theirs. Is it OK to take that fourth week when everyone else only seems to take three? There's no need for you to be in the office that week, but maybe you should stay anyway so people don't think you're permanently on holiday?

If you recognize this thought process, or worse, have answered yes to any of the above questions, or even more alarming, have actually changed behavior in a situation like this—don't feel guilty! Please. Read on and learn how.

You Are Normal—
a Normal, Guilt-Obsessed Woman

Christy Runningen, a Best Buy corporate talent coach in Minnesota, learned just how destructive and hard to shake guilt can be, even though she is one of the lucky ones. She's working in what Best Buy calls a ROWE—a Results Only Work Environment. It's the brave new world we mentioned in chapter 2 and that we'll explore further in chapter 7—where time on the clock has become irrelevant, and all that is measured is output. A mother of three young children, and someone who struggled with capricious bosses for years, Christy has seen her life transformed by ROWE. But, she says, the hardest part of making even this fully sanctioned flexible situation work has been changing the guilt-inducing voices in her head.

> *"I'm guilty of wanting to be that supermom. Even my mom gets on me like, 'Relax, you don't have to be the best at everything you do.' But I don't want people at work to start saying 'Oh well she's got kids, so she isn't really going to be performing well, or she's got graduate school so I guess she can't handle all of that stuff at once.' And I had felt the need to prove to everybody that I can do it all, you know, I've got straight As in my Master's in psychology, and I'm doing well at work, and I'm trying to be a supermom and all of this other stuff. So it's been gradual for me to get to the point where if I have to leave work early I don't worry whether people are looking at me funny."*

Listen to all of that. It's just an incredible waste of time. Think about all of the time you sit around obsessing like Christy, wondering what the "right thing" is, what your boss or colleague or whoever might think, instead of focusing on getting your work done or hanging out with your family. It eats up our minds, and it saps our energy. Enough.

We put some of the most guilt-ridden and guilt-conquering female minds to the task of developing a method of getting over time-consuming guilt. Almost all of us agreed that the onset of unreasonable guilt is like an emotional attack— something that gains its own momentum and is driven by its own logic. Fending off any attack requires that you gain the initiative, which means you need to quickly identify what's going on and then confront it. Our Guilt Bashers help you head off guilt fast.

Guilt Bashers

Guilt is a sneaky emotion. Unlike anger, love, or sorrow, it has an ability to work behind the scenes without your really noticing. This means that you first need to identify that it's actually there—that the undercurrent of emotion behind this flurry of negative, self-blaming thought is guilt. From there, the steps toward getting guilt out of your thought process and daily life are relatively simple.

STEP 1   ASK THE RIGHT QUESTIONS

You first need to identify what's going on. You're feeling as if you did something wrong. But did you? Ask yourself:

1. Did I actually lie, deceive, or really let someone down?

Maybe you're having some healthy guilt—which is really more like remorse. If so, and the situation is already in the past, do something about it, and then please, MOVE ON. Send a card, write an e-mail, make a call. Apologize, explain, whatever. Get it out of your mind and put it someplace else. Dwelling on it doesn't help anyone, and most importantly, it takes up your precious time.

2. Am I guilty of guilt exaggeration?

Often a feeling of guilt is justified, but its response is blown out of proportion. Imagine someone doing to you what you're feeling guilty about. Nine times out of ten, you'd probably say to yourself, "Yeah, that wasn't the best thing they could have done, but it definitely wasn't the worst either. I'll get over it, so should they."

3. Am I suffering from inappropriate guilt?

Most of the time, we reckon you are. Perhaps your boss is suggesting, even though you are supposed to be off on Friday, or at a lunch, or coming in late, that it would be helpful for you to cancel your plans and pitch in with someone else's project. You're feeling queasy and guilty. You start down that familiar path, hearing that well-worn internal dialogue with yourself that can spiral into nuttiness. "Oh, I should probably give up my day off or my lunch hour or my trip this weekend." "I was wrong to ask for that day off, time at my son's school, a late morning." "My boss clearly believes I'm a slacker, lazy, or lack ambition." "I'm letting down my boss, the team, my gender." "Maybe I'll lose my job, my respect, my identity."

When you are starting to spin this way, learn to recognize it before you get dizzy with guilt. If you can identify the onslaught, you are already on your way to having a healthier emotional life. You can see what is inappropriate. The day, lunch hour, weekend off was yours. You will lose time if you give it up.

"I'm getting so much better at recognizing that part of this is my own thing," says Linda Brooks, the New York lawyer. "The paranoia and self-talk that says 'I shouldn't be doing this. I should be available 24/7.'"

If you are having trouble sorting out whether the guilt is justified, then getting to the source of the "should" can help. Remember this: guilt is one of the basic human emotions that people in public or professional life will use to get you to do what they want. It's a very sharp, very sophisticated emotional tool— one that bosses love to wield. The explanation is simple: in situations where you're entitled to your break, to your vacation, to asking someone else to do a project, your boss knows that it's unreasonable to take away that right. So that's where he uses guilt to get what he needs.

Avoiding this kind of tactical guilt—which you might otherwise call "bosses' guilt"—is a matter of breaking down any feeling of "should" into *legitimate* shoulds, where you actually failed to fulfill your obligations, and *illegitimate* shoulds, where you had no business fulfilling a request in the first place.

Lauren Tyler, a private equity banker at a top New York firm, who some days seems to be managing a small circus as she handles her high-level job, three children, and two stepchildren, says her industry thrives on an all-or-nothing competitive spirit. "You have to develop a thick skin. I know I'm doing my job well and I don't have time to angst," she says. "It's not always easy, but I've learned to get things done in my business life and my personal life, without a lot of hand-wringing."

So ask yourself: is the guilt you are feeling at a particular moment serving you and your own moral framework, or is it serving someone else and their wants and needs? If you come to the conclusion that you're being guilted so someone else can gain, throw the guilt away.

STEP 2   WRITE IT ALL DOWN

Early in the guilt-bashing, time-winning process, you will find that thinking is not enough. It will be hard to hear all of those familiar guilt thoughts and unfamiliar guilt-conquering thoughts and make sense of them. So get out that pen again.

1. List exactly what you believe you should feel badly about. Your personal classic guilt trips. All of them.

2. Stare at the list. Now, on another sheet of paper, make another list. A list of guilt busters. All the things you should feel good about. (That rarely occurs to any of us, of course.) Examples: "I asked for the day off." "People are allowed to have days off in the company." "I am only going to lunch, not to China." "I've been doing a great job lately on the Brenner report." "My boss is not going to dwell on this—he's got a lot more to think about." "Managers usually try to get all they can from people, and when they fail, they move on." "It's his job—it's not personal. " "He does not think I'm a bad person." "I'm going to seem more powerful for sticking to my plan."

You see where we are going here. We're reminding you how to keep things in perspective. Eventually we should be able to do it without the help of exercises. But sometimes we need to stop our minds from spinning, put it all on paper, and have a look. It really does help.

STEP 3   PICTURE YOUR BOSS IN DIAPERS

Think of bosses as crying, whining children who need a bit of discipline. Forgive the analogy, but it is really quite similar to training little ones. The first time a tantrum or refusal to go to bed crops up, or, let's say, an unreasonable work request is made, you will feel horrible and guilt-ridden at "letting down" your child/boss. But once you power through the tears/pressure, which lasts much less time than you imagine, you'll soon realize you've gained power. You've set not only boundaries but also a precedent for the future. Further, you'll wonder why you didn't try it a long time ago. The next time, your child/boss will cry/demand less. The time after that, they might not whine/make an unreasonable demand at all. And you've got power—not to mention a tension-relieving inside giggle at your supervisor.

STEP 4 CHANGE THE SOUNDTRACK

Pretty soon, you can drop all of the paper and lists and funny mental images and do it all reflexively. You'll easily understand where your mind is going BEFORE you start to spiral. Then you're really saving time. You can cut off the whole long-winded, emotionally draining process at the start, and move on.

Another way to think about it when these negative thoughts crop up: you need to literally change the "thought-track" in your head. Change your internal message. Instead of running a negative track about all of the things you haven't done and the reasons why you have to meet unreasonable requests or you might be forever doomed, you turn on the positive track, which reminds you of all of your accomplishments and power. If you keep that on a continuous loop, then your angst will float away.

Christy Runningen of Best Buy says the only way she stops it is by literally forcing her mind onto better terrain. "It's so easy to get overwhelmed and think, 'oh I should be doing this, or I should be doing that,' or 'I feel guilty, it's ten o'clock on a weekday morning and I'm not working at this very moment,' Christy says. "Well for me the key is backing up and taking a look at what I am responsible for. It doesn't matter if I'm not doing it at this very second. I'm meeting every work goal, and that's what matters."

STEP 5   COMPROMISE COUNTS

There are times when you will feel unreasonable guilt, and you should not have to "give in," but the reality is that you won't always get to do things your way. Don't always focus on an all-or-nothing outcome. That in itself can create lots of tension. At these moments, instead of letting your guilt force a dejected "cave-in," look for a split. You may be able to get part of what you want. "I can't come in Friday because I've already made plans, since I asked for the day off last month, but I can work through my lunch today. I hope that helps!" This sort of olive branch seems powerful, can leave you feeling good, and still preserves the basics of what you need. And when you do have to compromise—for goodness' sake don't feel guilty about doing so. You haven't sold yourself short or failed, you've just compromised! You've lost some time during your lunch break but at least you've won your Friday.

STEP 6   PULL OUT THE RHETORICAL GUILT SHIELDS

We tend to think silence and a smile are the best guilt-deflectors, but if you just can't help yourself, here are some ready-made scripts you can use to avert an assault from coworkers and bosses.

"Out the door so early," your annoying coworker sneers.
"It's awesome how quickly I nailed that Brenner report," you reply with a smile.

"I was at the office until midnight last night," grumbles your office mate, pointedly.

"Brutal," you sympathetically reply. "When I logged on at 6 A.M. this morning, I thought I'd die."

"This project could really use your input over the weekend—oh— did you say you were away?" your boss asks, clearly testing the waters.

"Absolutely—I agree it should not go out without my once-over. I'll have it done Monday midday."

No—Just Say It

Once you've tamed your inner-guilt monster, you are ready to welcome that most wonderful of words into your vocabulary. We're certain you barely use it. But it's a potent combination of two letters that could routinely save our sanity. Go ahead. Say it. You know the word we mean.

NO.

Are we simply allergic to it, terrified of the consequences? What do we really think will happen if it becomes a regular part of our speech? Maybe the world would be rocked by an Armageddon of hurt feelings? Perhaps our pictures would be blasted through cyberspace as modern-day Leona Helmsleys? Or worst of all, people might be—*disappointed?*

Maybe. But here's the fundamental problem. When we are so eager to please everyone and avoid people being cross with us, we end up saying yes to a lot of things we don't really want. This of course means we end up spending more time working than we really want. And that's why you are reading this book.

"In the past I tended to be a 'yes 'person," Stephanie Hampton, the Marriott spokesperson told us. "I'd say 'yes' to just about anything and everything, in the belief that I was building a reputation for myself as a can-do, go-to person. I looked around and noticed that a lot of successful people don't say 'yes' to everything; they are more strategic. They say 'yes' for a variety of reasons. True, sometimes it's based on who's doing the asking. But most of the time successful people choose to say 'yes' to strategic or value-added work. So now I think about whether a project will put 'heads on beds' or otherwise enhance the brand reputation of Marriott. If the answer is no, it's usually just busywork, and I try to find a way to say 'no' without saying 'no.'"

Our New York lawyer, Linda Brooks, says she still backslides. "I think people don't like to be told no, so I have to get a thicker skin and resist the urge to please everyone, because I sit there and think, 'oh my God he hates me now,' and 'he's never going to give me another deal' and 'I'm sure the partners are going to vote next week to kick me out of the partnership because I said "no" to that deal.' My head goes there. So it does take a bit of thickening of the skin. But it does get easier."

You may not believe it now, but tossing off *no* will become second nature. It's a must-have tool for implementing Womenomics. You'll see in the upcoming chapters how much use it gets. Once you've really set your goals, you will be much clearer about what you want to tackle and what you don't want to take on. It gets refreshingly simple actually—that weekend assignment, no; those extra hours, no; that promotion with all the travel and increased responsibility, no. You will learn not just to say "no," but also to think no, mean no, and act no.

And yes, employing it may mean you disappoint, anger, and annoy. But it will also mean you are happier, healthier, and more straightforward. It's certainly a better situation for you and, also, therefore, for everyone in your life in the long run. Even the recipients of your nos!

CLAIRE I've always been an ardent people pleaser. For some reason, I grew up with the sense that saying yes as much as I can is more important than anything else. Disappointing people, letting them down—just the thought of that can send me into guilt spasms for days. I came to believe that being thought of as a "nice" person was the ultimate achievement. And I still believe that compassion and caring are at the top of my list. But I've also come to understand that my "yes" behavior could be intensely frustrating and stressful to me, my family and friends, and the people getting my "yesses." I was constantly taking on more than I could handle—and then having to back out of projects or commitments—making the very people I was trying to help angrier than they would have been in the first place after just hearing a "no." Once my son was born, I started to understand that I had to cut back on my people-pleasing, since I had someone who wanted and needed my attention so much, and he was clearly my priority. But I was still trying to do too much until one incident radically changed my outlook. I'd said yes to a trip out west for a story that I knew was not a top priority, but I didn't want to "let down" the senior producer who'd asked me. I was juggling other projects, one of which then went on the air to tepid reviews. On top of that, my husband and I had barely seen each other, and my son was quite clingy. I came back from the trip with my typical chest cold, which my doctor finally told me she believed was stress-induced, since I managed to get it seven or eight times a year. I spent two days limping around the house, fighting with my husband instead of having a nice weekend with him as we'd planned, and I was too sick and tired to go to my son's first swimming lesson. And I finally had to tell the senior producer I just could not finish her project, which had her livid, to say the least. It was an ugly period, for sure, but a critical awakening for me about the power, and the necessity, of no.

We'll walk you through some very situation-specific ways to say "no" in chapters 5, 6, and 7. But first, you must have the psychological grounding, the mental readiness to deploy this powerful instrument without fretting about what people think of you when you use it. You really will come to believe that no is not negative. It's as positive as it gets.

Recognizing a *NO* Moment

You probably already have a very good internal radar as to what constitutes a reasonable request and what does not; what is part of your job, and what is inappropriate. It's funny how we all know immediately *after* we say yes that we made the wrong move. How many times have we said: "Why did I say yes to that?" We knew beforehand too. You just have to become a better sleuth.

Asking yourself these questions will help you make a rational evaluation of the consequences at work. They dig inside your emotions to get to your gut instinct—which is almost always right but just hard to uncover.

The best opening question to ask yourself is, very simply:

"Does this request help me in any way?"

If you realize that the request is completely unhelpful to you, then you've got a definite *no* moment on your hands. You might have to figure out *how* to say "no" (see the sections below) but the *no* should be said.

If the request actually does have value to you, and can be

helpful to you, then there are a few follow-up questions to ask yourself. First, try to calibrate the importance of the request in terms of a bigger picture by asking:

"Will this make a big difference to my career?"

In many cases the answer will be that, no, it doesn't. And here you also need to factor in smaller questions such as—do I actually have the time and the skills necessary to do it well? Otherwise, it could have a *negative* impact on your career! But you might also find that you believe that it *is* important to your career, and that you can pull it off. You've no doubt learned by now that if something is going to affect your career, then it's bound to affect other things in your life. And, thus, the next question:

"How will this affect my balance at home?"

Be honest here. You may know you have a tendency to fear the worst, and assume every change in your schedule will be a personal tsunami, leaving your children whiplashed and virtually orphaned. Or you may typically assume you can handle everything, only to see it all come crashing together in an ugly way later. Know yourself, know your tendencies, and think through what you really think will happen.

Lauren Tyler fairly pulsates with a welcoming, magnetic energy. Her nature is one of the things that make her so successful, but at the same time it's something she's come to understand can leave her overburdened and a target of unnecessary requests. She's spent twenty years honing her process of reaching no, and keeps it simple with a variation on the above three questions. "At this point I always ask, 'Does it help me do my job? Or does it help my kids?' If the answer is no, I don't take it on."

Robin Ehlers of General Mills easily weeds out the obvious nos with the above questions, but she has also learned to recognize that there are things she's inclined to turn down because they seem daunting, but which she actually enjoys, professional and personal. "Even if it seems hard and it might be disruptive, is it something that I'll actually enjoy doing in the end? That's what I try to figure out," she says. "Like Monday night I had thirty people over for this charity dinner, and I was like, 'I can't believe I did this.' But I actually enjoyed it, and I've also learned not to worry about the house looking perfect or the food being great."

That moves us toward asking the more personal questions. They deal with your instinct, your gut feeling, your intuition, your sixth sense. Think of them as an emotional litmus test.

"Do I have a feeling in the pit of my stomach when I think about saying yes?"

If there is that unpleasantly nervous feeling—something more than just "butterflies"—then you need to stop and figure out what's going on, since this is an emotional red flag. The fact that you can physically feel the pit lingering there is an indication of how strong your doubt is.

"Will I be mad at myself for saying yes instead of no?"

If you have an inkling that you'll be angry or feel some kind of resentment toward yourself, then you should seriously consider saying "no," since any self-directed anger indicates a feeling of self-betrayal.

Lastly, make sure that you actually feel positive about the request:

"Am I eager to do this at all? Does any of it appeal to me?"

Here's where looking back to the past for clues, which is what Robin does, can be helpful. Are there other situations where you've thought something might be hard, or unwise, and then in the end you actually were happy you said yes? Part of this, again, is knowing yourself well and recognizing when your re- action is simply a fairly meaningless habit, or actually consti- tutes real warning bells.

Gear Up for the No

In time, the detective work that will lead to a decision about saying yes or no will become much easier. And obviously, there's no standard formula to use to reach that decision. We can't tell you that if you respond a certain way to five out of those six ques- tions, for example, you should shout "Forget it!" at the top of your lungs. But we do know that with practice, and by constantly using those questions as an evaluating tool for each potential *no* situation, making a certain kind of decision will start to feel natural. Eventually, it will be fluid and even unconscious, in the sense that you'll be able to perceive all the important elements, all the positives and negatives on the field, in the blink of an eye. Your nos (and, accordingly, your yesses) will be confident, un- hesitating, and forward-moving.

But this does take practice. Fortunately, there's a relatively easy way to train for the no, and it doesn't require you to rapid- fire that two-letter word at your boss until it feels natural.

The *No* Workout

- Think about all of the recent nos you've received. Can you even remember them? Were you really devastated? Are you still thinking about them? Probably not. Remember, anticipation is always worse than reality.

- Keep a list handy of all of your commitments. That's what Robin Ehlers does. "It's the easiest way to be strong," she laughs. If you made a list in the guilt section, pull it out. Keep a copy at work and at home, even in your wallet. Look at it when somebody is making a request of you. It makes turning things down much easier.

- The moment someone next makes a request, think to yourself, "Absolutely not." Just think it. Even if you may say yes later. It will help to set your boundaries.

- Never say yes simply to avoid conflict, or to move on. Never. It makes things horribly complicated later. If you really don't have the time or desire, and you may have to say no later, you are making things far worse. Doing a bad job, or letting someone down later, is much more damaging. Think of this as a time-management issue. You are not lazy but merely being professional. "I've become a big believer in being absolutely direct," explains Lauren Tyler. "I respond quickly to e-mails, phone calls, and with my nos. People don't need their time wasted."

- Look around the office for *no* role models—people you've noticed who deliver *no* well. Don't hesitate to pinch their techniques. Also look around the office and think about which people you have the hardest time turning down. Think about why and devise new techniques for dealing with them.

The Womenomics-Approved *No*

The key to this kind of no is the delivery, since you're trying to communicate a very clear message in an inoffensive way. It's a difficult task, but it's doable. The things to remember, which will always serve you well:

Mind your manners: Make good eye contact, smile, be friendly. Remember, you are saying no. You can afford to be gracious.

Keep it clear: If the request is unclear, ask for immediate clarification. "What are you asking exactly?" "Who else might be able to do it?" "Who will be able to help?" Keep it all crisp, and speak in an objective, information-gathering tone.

Take your time: It's always OK to buy time, especially while you get used to this new state of affairs. "Let me think about it and go over my obligations and get back to you." "I can't talk right now; I'm on the other line. Can I call you back?" You will often say a better no or yes if you have enough time to think. Just remember: if you decide to say "no," don't hesitate. Any hesitation leaves an opening for the person making the request.

Keep it simple: The fewer words the better. Ideally, we could all get by with a simple no and turn and walk away, à la Clint Eastwood. That's the real power move, but in our experience, it's unrealistic. So we've come up with a more nuanced *no*, which we've come to call our

NO SANDWICH

(You'll soon be addicted!)

ON TOP

Breezy and sincere apology or praise

"I wish I could help." "Ordinarily I'd love to." "That's just what I'd want to do."

THE FILLING

Crisp, plain hearty NO meat

" I have other obligations/deadlines/plans/meetings."

"My schedule won't let me take that on."

THE BOTTOM

An alternative

"What about Tuesday/next week/Carrie Logan/hiring a temp?"

"I could assign Bert to that if you like."

Plans. Have them. A lot of them. We love this method. Remember, saying you have plans, the filling layer of our sandwich, does not mean you are engaged away from home, or even at an office event. Having plans can mean a date with your favorite book or TV show, dinner with the kids, or an afternoon of lying around. You don't owe anyone the details. Use it constantly.

Cite a policy. If you need more help finding good *NO* filling for your sandwich, it can help to come up with a set of personal policies. They can be handy comebacks for both personal and work requests on your time. "Oh, I wish I could, but we have a family policy that we don't go out during the week," or "Friday night is our movie night, I'm sorry." Even for work requests: "I make it a policy never to travel more than once a week. Will next week work?" "Our family policy is no business breakfasts until the children are out the door to school. What about 9 A.M. coffee?"

Policies sound official, and even citing a family policy at work makes you seem organized and thoughtful. Further, it can make the no less personal and random. You are not saying "no" to the person—but rather blaming the policy. It can remove the sting. And best of all, you may find it actually helps you come up with a better set of priorities!

The diplomat's no: There are many ways to say "no" that don't require you to actually utter those two fatefully combined letters. You should be able to say "no" outright, if that's how you feel, but the truth is that sometimes you won't have that confidence. And other times, the diplomat's no is simply part of a more effective strategy.

You can also think of it as a burden shift. It's actually a critical part of the bottom layer of our NO Sandwich. It's ideal if you can say yes to part of the request, and no to part—then you get credit for being a "yes" person, but you get to handle things more on your terms. Using a time frame is often your answer. "I'd love to. I'd be able to get it to you three weeks from Monday. Will that work?" "Absolutely, you'll have it tomorrow. But I'll have to give you the Condon account next week. I assume that's OK?"

"I often say 'I'd love to help, but these are my priorities right now,'" says Christy Runningen. "'Can I get back to you next week with this piece of it? Here's what I'm up against, so can we push this part of it to Thursday?'" It's honest, and it shows you're trying to compromise and often can encourage them to find other solutions."

Robin Ehlers often likes to rely on her "calendar."

"Just the other day, somebody called me from Minneapolis and said we're taping this segment on one of our food products on November 14th and wanted to make plans for me to be there.

I just told her, 'You know, I'll look at my calendar and see if I can work it in with some other appointments and let you know.' And it's one of those things in my mind I went through like this: 'Okay, so what's the big deal about me being there? Yes, I should be there as a representative for General Mills, but I'm not going to get any business for it. You know, I might meet some people at the station, but there's nothing there for me down the road.' So I just kind of walked through and decided I probably won't go unless I can tie in something else valuable with that."

Here's our New York lawyer's version of the diplomat's no:

"'Oh, I would love to. Oh my God, that sounds so interesting. I wish I could, let me think about that and get right back to you.' Then I call them back and I say, 'No, I can't.'"

Christy Runningen also likes questions.

"Whenever I get that cringing feeling inside as I start to hear an overwhelming request, the first thing I usually ask is: 'Why do you need my help? What is it that you're trying to get to?' I have a master's degree in psychology, and so I tend toward questions. And often we find out together that there's another solution."

KATTY   This is a really hard one for me. I hate the idea that people won't like me, so I'll bend over backward to accommodate and please people. I'm also terrible at confrontation, and you don't need a PhD in psychology to see the two are related. I used to avoid saying no to people, but now with four kids and a job I've just had to force myself to do it. I'm still not very good at the bald-faced NO though. I still fear the negative reaction that it will provoke. So I get around it by dressing up my nos in soft language. I don't have the confidence yet to say, "No, and by the way you were out of order even asking that," so I'll say, "That sounds like an interesting opportunity, but I'm afraid I have too many commitments." I should work on the blunt NO, though—I think it would ward off further requests.

Take the bull by the horns: Once you make your decision, it's yours to fight for. You've gone through all the processing, probably some soul-searching, and you've found the answer to what once seemed like a Sphinx's riddle. So, go after it with confidence. Don't water down the delivery with problem language like "I think . . ." or "maybe if . . ." or "I'm unsure about . . ." You'll get trapped!

Say it early: Be active about any no, once you see it's in range. Again—being definite and firm makes you seem organized, in charge, and on the offensive.

CLAIRE   I'd been envisioning this particular train crash for months, and it would knot up my stomach every time I thought about it. The Republican National Convention was conveniently scheduled for the first week of September 2008, coinciding exactly with the first week of school for both of my children, then three and six. My husband had to be at the convention too, but even if he could have stayed home, I would have wanted to be at home to help with the emotional preparation for both kids entering new classes. I think most parents know getting ready for that first day, and being there when they get home to hear the tales of excitement or woe, is critical parent time. In my mind, I'd decided there was simply no way I could be away. But I also knew ABC would almost certainly expect me to be at the convention. Finally, I decided to jump in BEFORE they started planning convention coverage. In late May, I sat down with the executive producer and told him bluntly there was an approaching issue. I told him I knew this could be a problem, but that there was simply no way I'd be able to go to the Republican convention for them. And I told him why, leaving no doubt about where I needed to be that week. Firm, but not combative, was my goal. He thought about it and mulled it over, thinking to himself who might go and what that would mean, and then he said, "We should be able to handle that."

I was walking on air the rest of the day. It was such a burden lifted from my shoulders. And I really believe because I got in there early, it made a difference. Had they already put me on a list and started planning work for me, they would have been more invested in my presence, and then it might have been a showdown.

The Beauty of Boundaries

Part of the beauty of saying "no" 'is that you're doing much more than staving off an unwanted assignment or a new responsibility or obligation. The rush of confidence and even the slightly otherworldly sense of well-being that arrives after a decisive *no* moment comes in part from the knowledge that you won't have to cram a round-peg assignment into the square hole of your schedule. But also, that feeling of calm mixed with pride is a feeling of moving forward as a person, of having grown a bit.

The reason why this feels empowering is that being able to say "no" when you mean it represents an ability to set boundaries. You can even see this by pegging your own growth as a person to the kinds of domestic and personal boundaries you've been able to establish over the years. While many of us have done a great job of setting boundaries at home—and especially if there are kids in the house who depend on having boundaries set for them—we've often neglected to transfer the same ability to our workplace. But boundaries at work are just as important as the ones at home, if only because what goes on at the office has such heavy repercussions on what goes on at home. Your bosses and your underlings need boundaries every bit as much as your five-year-old. The clarity helps their decision making and their ability to work well, and in the long run it will generate enormous respect for your maturity.

And best of all, it's a reinforcing behavior. Think of each no as a small dot—part of a bright line you are drawing around your life and priorities. Each no not only makes the next easier, but it also starts to ensure you'll have to say them less often. You'll come to understand this even better in chapter 6, where we discuss in detail the many benefits to your professional reputation that *NO* offers. Saying "no" will make you seem more confident. When you put a value on your time, and you are clear about it, others will see your time as valuable too. A healthy distance from guilt, and a healthy use of *no* will ensure you are respected. And in the end, respect is far more valuable to you at work than being liked.

A Twist of Obligation

Lots of women, ourselves included, dread saying "no" because of the tangle of emotions that we discussed above. For many women, there is an added barrier to the self-affirming no: it's the social, or maybe we should say sociological, obligation.

Melissa James understands the emotion of sociological obligation as well as anyone. Melissa is a rare individual in many ways. She's one of the few African American women who have risen to the upper echelons at investment banking powerhouse Morgan Stanley. In fact, she's one of only a small group of African American women in the whole cutthroat, macho financial industry to have reached those kinds of professional heights.

Beyond her professional achievements, Melissa also managed to get smart about her life, about balance. To speak in the language of this book, she managed to change her perspective and came to look at her life and job through the Womenomics lens. At one point early in her career, she took the initiative, sat down with her boss, and asked for "more flexibility." After explaining what she had in mind by that somewhat ambiguous two-word phrase, her boss said something mildly shocking: "That's great." They had no intention of losing her.

She's since moved back to full-time work as the global head of loan products for the company, but she remembers that at the time, it wasn't bosses' guilt or professional self-doubt that she had to deal with. For the most part, it was something else.

"I think there are a whole bunch of issues about being a minority of any kind," Melissa told us.

"Whether you're a minority by virtue of your gender, or by virtue of your ethnicity or whatever, there are issues. There's more baggage, there are more challenges, there are more obstacles. It's more difficult in certain respects. Maybe it's easier in others, but on the whole it's more difficult. And you can feel a greater sense of obligation to achieve or to do things well, like, 'I have to do things well because I am such a rarity, or I'm doing this for the entire race, or all African American women, or whatever, so I can't give in now.'"

Think about this for a minute. Melissa is a person who had overcome all the odds to get to where she wanted to be. Not only this, but she also had managed to take control of her life, get time off, pare down her workload, and still remain a valuable player at a high-stakes financial firm. And yet, she still felt guilty.

Women's emotional waters run deep. Melissa, despite years of hard work and substantial, traditionally defined success, didn't become the ball-busting corporate ice queen that you see in the movies. After jumping (or, in her case, leaping) the professional barriers, she went on to face personal ones—years of troubled pregnancies and negotiations about work-life balance. After getting past the personal barriers she went on to focus on her obligations to society as a whole. But she emerged the victor.

"I'm extremely happy about where I am," she told us, "and that is not to say that I have everything I want or there is something that is ideal or that is perfect or that there's not angst or ambivalence, but when I look at things in the scheme of my own life and I look at the success that I've enjoyed and the seniority that I have, the responsibility that I have, the money that I get paid, the whole package of workplace flexibility that I have, this package really works for me."

We couldn't dream of a better example than Melissa James of what can be achieved, both professionally and personally, with the right approach. Melissa, and all the rest of us, need only go one step further: instead of feeling an obligation to do more and more, we need to turn that driving emotion toward feeling pride for what we've already done. Instead of feeling guilty, as we imagine what our female predecessors might think about our choices to scale back the work hours, or what our ethnic community or even family might think, we need to understand that most of those people would be awed by what we've already accomplished, which is that we've earned the ability to decide. Exercising this ability means saying "no" when you need to and not falling into a guilt trap for doing so. And, in fact, exercising this ability will help to build a world our successors will be thankful for.

Over the next three chapters, we're going to map out the path to building this world for you—the world of work-life freedom—from the baby steps of buying minutes in your day to the gigantic strides of completely overhauling your work deal.

We'll start small and accessible. There are things you can do today, with no confrontations or meetings or favors asked, to win yourself more time. We'll look at your home lives and your work lives to see how you can cut tasks down and be more efficient. Then we'll get strategic and, yes, psychological again, and look at how you can buy freedom for yourself and help your employer with an attitude change. You'll learn, for example, to pick those plum assignments to maximize your impact and the company's benefit. And then we'll talk about how to really renegotiate the whole deal. How you can plunge in and shake off the tyranny of nine-to-six, or eight-to-seven, or seven-to-nine, or whatever your personal prison is, once and for all.

news you can use

1. Guilt is a useless emotion that keeps you from achieving work-life sanity.

2. Changing the guilt soundtrack in your head will open the door to a powerful, life-changing little word: No. It's one you need in order to master Womenomics.

3. If you don't say "no" to some things you will end up doing everything.

lazy like a fox: work smarter not harder

Work smarter, not harder—a concept as simple and elegant as $e = mc^2$. Einstein's equation changed the world; our foolproof Womenomics formula will change your universe. What they have in common is a new understanding of energy. If you're going to work less and still achieve, you need to understand where to direct your precious energy resources. Remember: your time and energy are finite commodities; you need to use them to maximum effect.

That's where our fox comes in. Foxes are precise and cunning, a disposition we applaud. They know instinctively how to sniff out the best opportunities, a skill that allows them to hunt when and how they want, but with minimum effort. They aren't given to wasting excess energy, but they do know when to put on a sudden spurt to maximize their chances of a kill, or an escape! This is an overarching and intrinsic aspect of Womenomics: you need to develop ways to get greater returns on the investment of your time.

Or think about it this way: you're shopping, and you have $300 to spend. Should you fritter it all away, as you roam around, on junky but captivating earrings and necklaces from street vendors, or should you focus on making that really big quality purchase of a knockout dress? That dress will get you more bang than the cheap but entertaining bling. It's the same with your time. It's a critical commodity.

The first major practical step to becoming smarter with your time is to rethink the relationship between time and productivity. Kathleen Christensen of the Sloan Foundation notes that the very idea of productivity measured by time on a clock is starting to look antiquated. "For a very long time the notion was that, the longer the hours you work, the more productive you are. And I think that there is an increasing awareness that it's not necessarily how long you work, but how smart you work. I have certainly seen cases where people have reduced their hours and stayed as productive."

Kathleen is exactly right in this respect, but even she could go one step further. It's not just *possible* to reduce raw hours and maintain (or even increase) your productivity—it's absolutely necessary. As you work smarter not harder, you'll see that your whole life will begin to improve. Reduced stress, a greater sense of fulfillment, fewer distractions, and less worry will continue to improve your productivity at work, and your improved results-oriented performance will, in turn, free up yet more time. Over the next three chapters, we'll show you exactly how to work smarter on the small stuff, the big stuff, and even on a newly negotiated flexible deal.

Chandra Dhandapani, our vice president at the financial giant Capital One, says her smart-time approach has won her enough time to relax with her husband and young son. "It's set off a positive cycle," she says. "I feel I'm a better person, and so I'm actually more engaged and productive at work, and then easier to work with!"

Smart time can even alleviate the need for part time. We know that the appeal of part-time work tempts all women, and it may sound like the natural solution to our "work less" quest. There's a romantic notion of the perfect three-day week, with time at home baking bread or constructing 3-D volcanoes or doing yoga. But remember, that formalized three-day week comes with a formalized three-day salary and three-day benefits. It's a big cut in your income. And all too often, as we all know, you find yourself doing the same work for less money. It might be right for you—and we have negotiating tips in chapter 7 that will help you should you go this route—but before you storm into your boss's office demanding fewer hours for less pay, why not try carving out time in your week by working smarter but for the same full-time salary?

This chapter is about how to start down the Womenomics path in easy, accessible ways. There are things you can do today, with no formal arragements, to win yourself more time. And you can change not only the quantity of time you have in your day but also the quality of your time. At home, at work, in the car—we're going to show you how to save time, to discover new reservoirs of untapped time, and most importantly, how to start living better, right now.

The 80–20 Rule

Keen business managers and analysts alike notice a strange but ultimately unsurprising trend—80 percent of useful output in business comes from about 20 percent of effort input. This rule, which is called the 80–20 Rule or, even more descriptively, the Law of the Vital Few, means that the average employee wastes almost 80 percent of her time in unproductive tasks or, just as likely, in trying to appear productive.

What this means for you is that on the one hand there are tasks that really change the bottom line, and on the other, tasks that basically do very little for you or for your company but that are extremly time-consuming. In all likelihood, you have already developed a built-in efficacy meter that allows you to gauge whether something will have a useful payoff or be a useless energy waster.

The trick, of course, is not just distinguishing between the useful and the useless but actually putting this knowledge to work. And you'll see throughout the next few chapters what this means in concrete terms, as you make judgments about which meetings, technology, and projects deserve your valuable time. More importantly, you'll come to see that it's your duty to yourself and your company to do things that will further your company's business in meaningful ways and not waste your time jumping through hoops just because the hoops are there.

So get out that pen and paper. It's list time again. Now we're tackling to-dos. And the first thing to remember—never ever ever do something simply because it's randomly placed on the top of a to-do list. Or because it seems the easiest to tackle. Your lists *must* reflect priorities.

First. Make a list of all of the things you are trying to accomplish in the next few days or weeks. Look at it. Accept that you cannot do everything. If the list has twenty things on it, circle those five that will have the highest impact. Remember to pick things that play to your strengths. If you know you won't do it well, don't take it on. And circle the few that are important for your professional satisfaction. Be realistic; there may be a few low-impact but necessary chores that have to stay on the list. If so, squeeze them in among the critical items. But cross the rest off.

Second. Write down your big-picture goal for the month— this is a concrete definition of something important you want to achieve this month, something that goes beyond your day-to-day tasks. Then write down ten things it will take to help you get there. Then pretend somebody is pointing a gun at you and you have to pick the top two actions. Focus on those two and those two alone.

Third. Write down your big-picture goal for the year. (This one is good for those of us who get lost in the trees.) And then break it down by month, by week, even by day. If your goal, for example, is to have ten new clients by the end of the year, break it down, each time listing the actions you can take to get there. Then simply make sure you are spending substantial time on those actions each month, each week, each day.

As you do this, remember that as overwhelming as it might seem, you have to think BIG as you make these priority lists. Remember to get out of the weeds. Otherwise, you'll be left juggling what other people hand to you, or tackling things on your list that seem "easy." While you might feel as if you are getting things done, in reality these small tasks simply eat up all of your time and potentially sabotage your career.

Linda Brooks, our New York lawyer, observes this tendency in women every day:

"I see a lot of women being what we call 'detail-oriented' and making sure that all the words on the paper are right, when a guy of similar seniority will not focus so much on the words but sit around thinking about bigger issues in a deal and trying to think outside the box, and doing all of that creative stuff. Guys step up to it much earlier and sometimes, frankly, too soon, and you have to smack them down and say 'Get the f***ing papers right, and then we can start talking about how to solve Exxon's balance sheet problem,' " she laughs. "It's funny, you'll see a guy who has been a lawyer for exactly three days really stepping up. And then you will see a woman who's been doing this for three years, and she's redoing the junior associate's paperwork because he didn't get it right. It happens all the time, it's so frustrating."

Robin Ehlers from General Mills thinks working according to smart priorities allows her a full-time job and plenty of freedom and time with her family

"Occasionally," she says, "I see that other people are working more 'frantically' than I am, but frankly, I think I just work smarter. I don't spend time on phone calls worrying about office politics, I don't waste time on meetings or hanging out at the office. I'm extremely bottom-line focused, and I think the company appreciates that. I really focus on the things that have to get done to move the business forward—and I don't really worry about a lot of the stuff that isn't value added."

Time-Trap Busters

Even once you've followed our advice and set your own priorities clearly, every day at the office, or even every day working at home, is a time-trap minefield. We all waste far too much time. So here are strategies that will keep you in full work-smarter mode. You might get the impression that we are awfully organized, with all this talk of lists and schedules and efficiency. Hardly. In fact we both naturally rebel against being scheduled or organized much at all. But we've come to realize that knowing how our day might run more effectively is critical to getting what we all want—more time at home.

1. Assume control of your schedule. This is an essential philosophical change. On every front and in every instance, you must take charge. If you leave it to other people to schedule meetings, phone calls, and work assignments, the chances are you'll end up working at times that suit them and not you. If you want to work on your schedule, take control of your timetable. And by the way, you have to take control of yourself as well. It's not just others mucking up your efficiency. Limit checking your e-mail and returning phone message to a few times a day. Schedule yourself big "think time" to get through the most important tasks.

2. Be the first to offer a deadline for work. As often as possible (and it probably is a lot more often than you think) *you* should dictate the timetable for an assignment deadline. Tell your boss early on when you will have your work completed. This lets you choose the schedule that will work best for you. But be realistic and don't promise the moon when you can't deliver it.

3. Be thorough—check out projects as if you are buying a used car:

- Don't be rushed into giving a timeline immediately. It is totally acceptable to reply by saying something like: "I'll look this project over and get back to you in the morning with a firm deadline."

- Evaluate how long the work will take: how many hours a day can you realistically give it?

- Do you have any other commitments that might create a conflict?

- How much extra time should you schedule as "budget padding" to deal with a mishap, lost document, sick team member, or other inevitable project hiccup?

4. Become an opportunistic workaholic. Whenever you see a window of opportunity—the kids are away, you have to travel anyway, your partner or parents don't need your help—go postal on work! Think of it as a chance to use foxlike cunning. These are golden opportunities to relive your old workaholic days but at very little cost.

"Exactly," agrees Robin Ehlers. "And you know what else I do? When I travel for work I take my office with me and I work the whole time I'm gone. I'll stay up really late, and I enjoy it. I feel like I'm caught up for the week, and then I can come back and have freedom."

5. *Put limits on your schedule.* Let people know when you'll be in the office, and be realistic and crisply assertive about it. If you've been traveling and want a few hours home in the morning the day after you get back, tell people, "I'll be in at midday." You need the time with family, and the world won't end because you are in a few hours late.

And start to make it plain to others in the office that when you are there, you are busy. Announce your "think time." Let everyone know when you'll be available to return calls or e-mails. You might even broadcast a rule that unless it's urgent, you'll be answering e-mails in the mornings and late evenings only. Such restrictions will simply make you seem organized and reinforce the message that your time is important.

Avoid the temptation to be the Hermione Granger–style star pupil and be constantly available. All too often we make promises in advance, reveling in the glow of our bosses' appreciation, and then wish, when the time comes, that we hadn't offered to be there for that early morning/late evening/weekend stint. And then we're not good employees.

CLAIRE   I used to avoid telling people when I'd be out of the office, even though my absence was sanctioned. I thought somehow it would draw attention to the fact I was not there. But I've come to realize it's much better for the people I work with to know my plans for the day, whether they want to be grumpy about them or not! I don't always say "I'll be sitting home in my sweats at the computer, then picking up my daughter after school, and then logging back in." They don't need that sort of detail. But I do now let people know "I won't be in tomorrow, I'll be on my cell phone, but I can have that script to you by 2 P.M." Or "I'm working from home—let me know if anything comes up, I'll be on my BlackBerry. This is the only time I can't be reached." It avoids tension and the sorts of situations where frustrated coworkers might say, "We had no idea where she was!"

6. *Mind your meetings.* What is it about these gatherings of office peers that suddenly give people the license to feel they can blather on endlessly and waste everybody's day? We're sure you've all sat through them. Those often totally unproductive meetings in an airless, windowless conference room where some office blowhard feels they can drone on and keep us stuck in the building when we're longing to get out the door.

Meetings are big time wasters. Here are a few tips for tweaking them.

Ask Yourself: Is It Necessary?

First and foremost, if it's not essential, don't go. Most of the time, you'll find, meetings will fall into that 80 percent category. They are useless. It's amazing how many meetings you can miss without it making any difference to how you do your job. It's equally amazing how quickly people get used to you NOT attending meetings and soon assume you won't.

KATTY   Every day we have a 10 A.M. and a 3 P.M. editorial meeting. When I took up my current job, my editor said it would be great if I could come along to them a few times a week. I said I'd probably try to call in. I'm afraid I lied. I've never attended any of those meetings either in person or by phone. And it really doesn't affect how I do my job. In fact my time is better spent reading reports and talking to contacts. And here's the real bonus: not going saves me at least an hour every day. If I have something to discuss that affects my reporting, I call or e-mail the editor directly. That takes five minutes instead of fifty.

CLAIRE   Ditto. We have hours of meetings and conferences at *Good Morning America*. Over time, I've realized it's more efficient for me, in my role as a reporter, not to participate all of the time. I now jump in when I've got something important I'm working on; otherwise, I get a synopsis at the end and use that extra time to actually report stories or do research or write.

Set and Control the Schedule

Sometimes you do just have to get people together in one place. When that is the case, try to take control of the meeting schedule. You be the one to announce the start time—and the stop time. If it's in a conference room that needs booking, you make the reservation and then keep the time short and meeting focused. Clarify goals with a written list in advance, to keep things on track. Even if you aren't in charge, jump in if you need to help keep things moving. "That's interesting—and what about our next question?" It will make you look smart and engaged, and serve your purpose.

Suggest a Conference Call Instead

For every busy woman, the conference call is a thing of *beauty*. Instead of allowing rogue minutes to escape as you travel to work, get to the meeting room, go through the chitchat rigma-role, and hang around for the postmeeting meeting, you can simply dial in from wherever you are and get going. Best of all is that you don't have to be present to be present: have a bite to eat, browse a document, or simply admire the view—and no one's the wiser. You may be able to talk from home so you don't have to waste time getting "office ready" (you know—hair, makeup, pressed jacket—all time-consuming stuff).

Over at Marriott the executive vice president of human resources is David Rodriguez. David has seen his company's business change dramatically. Unfortunately not all of his managers, the older ones in particular, are changing at the same warp speed. They cling to the 1980s way of doing business—meetings in meeting rooms, people sitting around a shiny conference table, minions to watch over. But in today's world that means they are missing an important skill.

"In the United States our lodging business is segmented into three large divisions: West, Central, East. Those regional teams are somewhere between twelve to fifteen people, and they rarely see one another. They're on teleconferences and constantly trav-eling," David explains. "If we had a senior manager who was uncomfortable with that, to me that would tell me he or she is not suitable to lead one of those teams, because you know some people have that attitude of 'I want all my staff surrounding me physically.' But that wouldn't meet the actual needs of the busi-ness. Because we need our people distributed."

So flexibility—the ability to teleconference and build and maintain relationships with virtual not-in-person communica-tion—is, for David Rodriguez, a positive asset. This is good news for anyone wanting to detach themselves from their desk. Your ability to be flexible, to function away from the office, is a business asset, and a time-saving gift.

The Two Faces of Technology

Technology truly is the leading enabler of today's increasingly flexible lifestyle. We professional women all know that without it, any flexibility we have would be almost impossible.

Conference calling from home means you don't have to be in the office at the crack of dawn to speak to London or stay there late at night to speak to LA. You can send e-mails as you wait in the carpool line. Your laptop allows you to have as much direct access to your work files as if you were sitting at your desk.

Kimberly Archer discovered the ultimate value of the Webcam when her third pregnancy threw her into enforced bed rest. At twenty-seven weeks' gestation, Kimberly, pregnant with twins, found she was at risk of premature labor. Her doctors sent her to bed, but Kimberly, who works for a professional recruitment firm, was determined to carry on her job. Technology was her savior. She knew she could e-mail, call, conference call, and tap into company files all from her laptop—but, stuck in her bed, she also discovered she could "meet" prospective candidates and employers just by dressing from the waist up and firing up her Webcam. They didn't see the crumbs and crumpled sheets— they just saw a professional woman in a smart jacket.

For Jennifer Dickey, the mechanical engineer in Detroit, technology allows precious time at home when there's an unexpected family call. "I can log on to my work computer from my home computer and it's just as if I was at work. The desktop looks the same, I have the same access to the same programs that I would have in the office. It helps greatly. For example, my daughter, who's three years old, is not one of those children who is excited about going to school every day. She still has rough days. So today I was an hour late to work. But I can make up that time one night this week by logging on to the computer after the kids have gone to bed and getting an hour's worth of work done then."

But these miraculous flexibility-enhancing gadgets can also sneak in and steal time away from us. So much of this techy stuff is self-service—and if you're like us, you can wind up in the middle of extremely frustrating evenings, trying to figure out how to get critical files off of a server. These gizmos need proper discipline or else they invade our personal lives with a vengeance.

"My son Jasper called my BlackBerry my new best friend once. That's when I realized I was really in trouble," Sarah Slusser confesses.

"I hear that checking your e-mails at night is an addiction. I know it was for me. If I had to get up at 3 A.M. to get a glass of water, I'd check my BlackBerry," Chandra at Capital One admits.

"On my day off I only check my BlackBerry four times a day," Stephanie at Marriott proclaims proudly—until she thinks for a minute and realizes she's talking about her day off!

Sound uncomfortably familiar? Ah, that shiny little handheld box—five inches long, half an inch thick. It is both the keeper and taker of our freedom. Our perfect personal assistant; our incessant, portable, professional conscience.

KATTY   I was years behind on the BlackBerry curve. I watched the "crackberry" addicts tapping over dinner and was appalled. I couldn't understand what could possibly be so urgent that they had to interrupt their salad to press send. I was pretty smug about my low-tech status and my self-imposed discipline. But sometime during the 2008 campaign the BBC decided enough was enough and they needed to be able to contact me while I was on the road. One Monday morning my producer handed me a BlackBerry. It sat in its packet for a week. But when I finally got round to using it I really was like an addict trying meth for the first time. I couldn't put it down. I checked my e-mails every ten minutes and soon was checking them evenings and weekends as well. I didn't "need" to for work, but somehow the fact that they were there, accessible in my purse, made me feel I had to. Soon my work was eating into my free time in a way it hadn't pre-BlackBerry.

CLAIRE   My BlackBerry is the key to being out of the office and with my kids when I need to be. I adore it. But between the hours of five and eight in the evening I've come to loathe it. I've noticed that I have a hard time putting it down during that critical dinner/bedtime hour, and that somehow when I get an e-mail from work—and they come fast and furious—I feel I need to respond instantly. Beyond that, those little messages almost act as tension transmitters. As I start to see what someone is asking me to do, my shoulders hunch, my mind gets into work-mode, and I'm suddenly ten times grumpier with my kids. Lately I've been simply putting it aside until after everyone is tucked into bed—and you can't imagine how much more relaxed I feel!

The perils of e-mail addiction are enormous. It can easily become a time abyss that kills your personal productivity, distracts you from your work, and even hampers creativity. You're not imagining this—there's research to prove it.

Consider the findings from the following three studies:

STRESSED-OUT?—STOP CHECKING YOUR E-MAIL!

Researchers at Glasgow and Paisley Universities in Scotland found in 2007 that e-mail, and its mismanagement, is a direct source of stress to employees. The study—completed

by a psychologist, a statistician, and a computer scientist—
showed that more than one-third of respondents feel
stressed by e-mail and the obligation to respond quickly.[45]

SLAYING YOUR PRODUCTIVITY—
E-MAIL, PHONE CALLS AND MINDLESS CONNECTIVITY

A 2008 study commissioned by the luxury car maker,
Cadillac, found that e-mails, phone calls, and mindless
Internet surfing result in up to four out of eight hours of
lost productivity each day![46]

LIGHT UP THAT DOOBIE—E-MAIL MAKES YOU STUPIDER.

Researchers at King's College London University found in
eighty clinical trials that trying to work—while checking
e-mails—temporarily reduces the IQ by ten points, the same
level of stupefaction caused by missing a night of sleep.
Consider that smoking marijuana causes only a four-point
temporary drop in functional IQ and you'll find that you're
better off getting stoned than checking your e-mail every
few minutes.[47]

But once you recognize that it's you who should control your
technology rather than the other way around, the process of asserting yourself can be remarkably easy and the benefits amaz-
ingly broad. When you pull the plug on your PDAs, the results
are instant. You will immediately gain more time. This is just as
critical *at* the office by the way. You'll find you can focus on the
big picture again. Most of the time spent on e-mails should be
relegated to the unnecessary 80 percent.

And controlling your use of PDAs off the job will help you
create a healthy separation from your workplace. Physically and

psychologically, you will be more relaxed and able to live in the present. You will focus better—on your family, on your kids. Even your friends will appreciate it. All those real people in your life will no longer be competing for attention with your unreal best friend, your BlackBerry. At the risk of sounding a bit New Age about this, we think you will be a better wife/daughter/mom/friend because you won't be distracted.

So, here are our simple ways to cut the addiction:

1. Turn off incoming e-mail alerts on your PDA and your computer's e-mail client. Don't think about doing this or consider doing this or ponder doing it—just do it. You'll find that not having a neurotic "ping" every few minutes will keep you from wasting time checking an e-mail whenever it shows up.

2. Do the 11/4 experiment. Studies have found that people are more productive, less stressed, and generally happier if they limit e-mail checking to twice a day— once at 11 A.M. and once at 4 P.M. You're probably thinking "Sounds great, but it'll never work for me." Try this once, for one day, and then get back to us on that (preferably not by e-mail).

3. If you're nervous that people will wonder where you are or what's going on, make the technology work for you by writing an autoresponder to the effect of: "Hi. I got your e-mail and will respond to you shortly during my e-mail checking hours which are 11 A.M. and 4 P.M."

4. Separate your technology. Keep your cell phone and your mobile e-mail device separate. Then you can take

breaks, leave your PDA and e-mails behind but still be able to call friends and family.

5. Leave the BlackBerry behind. Going out for dinner, a date, a movie? Remind yourself you can check it when you get back. Even an important meeting with a client or a brainstorming session will benefit from your full attention.

6. If you can't trust yourself not to check your PDA when it's in your purse or next to your bed, put it somewhere else. Literally leave that PDA at the other end of the house, move it up a flight of stairs. During the time it takes you to walk over and get it you have time to consider—why am I checking this? Do I really need to? The physical distance can help you unplug.

7. Set clear technology limits. Don't check your e-mails after 7 P.M. Don't check them during mealtimes. Don't check them more than once a day on weekends. Once you've decided you're not checking e-mails or taking work calls, simply turn off the phone, BlackBerry, or computer.

Changes on the Home Front

If you are going to work *and* have a family *and* have a life, then something has to give in every area of your existence, not just at work. It doesn't make sense to cut back your work to 60 percent and still try to manage your home life at 100 percent. The whole point of Womenomics is to get everything integrated, in balance, to be free not just from the tyranny of professional perfection but from the tyranny of domestic perfection as well.

Again, this book is not a parenting guide; if you're like us you've got too many of those already. But there are certain areas of your home life where you can apply the rules of Womenomics in order to win more time and freedom. Much of the mental and practical legwork that goes into redefining success at work needs to happen here too.

First off, you do not need to be supermom to be a *super* mom.

KATTY   I'm afraid I never go to PTA meetings. I confess I don't always make back-to-school night. I'm famous for forgetting half days and I have never been a room parent. The only Halloween costumes I have ever made by hand were so embarrassingly bad my kids refused to wear them. But I do make it a priority to have time at home so that I can be with my children when they need me. I'm not great at school events but I do make as much time as I can for homework, chatting about their days, negotiating tricky friendships and, recently, dispensing unwanted, and probably rather hopeless, advice on dating.

CLAIRE   I've spent two years in a row devoting long December evenings and generating bloody fingers to prove to my son (or myself, or somebody) that I could sew our Christmas stockings. When Hugo noted this year, as he struggled to pull his goodies from Santa out of my bizarre creation with an impossibly narrow top, that the shape might be a "little off," I realized I should stick to my strengths. Sewing? Maybe not so much. Build a cardboard house—I'm there. I've made a conscious effort to participate in the school

activities that will mean something to my son and daughter. A chance to come read to a class, or go on a field trip, I
adore that, and they get a kick out of it. But running a
parent group or an auction or helping in the library—I have
to rule those out —without guilt.

Whether it's in your social life, your kid's life, your extracur-
ricular life, or any other bit of your life, set limits. We are big
advocates of free time—literally lay-about time. Time with nothing scheduled. If you manage to tone down your work life only
to clog up the time you gained with other things, you've missed
the point. A few thoughts on managing the home front:

Our dos . . .

- Do schedule time just to hang out at weekends. Try to get
  through half a day without attending an organized activity.
  Remember that in a busy, fast-paced family, doing nothing
  is actually doing something. Give it a try and watch as the
  family does something rare and strange—relax.

- Do feel free to cancel evening engagements. It's fine to
  say, "I'm sorry I can't make it after all."

- Do feel free to say "I have 'plans,'" when plans are a movie
  with the kids or a family spaghetti dinner. We mentioned
  this in chapter 4; and it's critical. Not only are those the
  best sorts of "plans," but your family also deserves a firm
  commitment.

- Do be there for the big things at school—the graduations,
  the holiday play, the parent-teacher conferences—but
  don't beat yourself up about missing the others.

- Do delegate family events—your husband can do parent-teacher by himself if you can't make it. Dads often benefit from Mom not being there.

And our don'ts . . .

- Don't try to see too many friends on weekends—you'll end up not concentrating on the ones you do see.

- Don't sign your kids up for more activities than all of you can comfortably handle—it's one more schedule to organize, and you and your spouse will spend your weekends playing chauffeur, separately.

- Don't let your job bleed into your free time because you've scheduled too many pseudosocial events. Whether it's benefits, office drinks, fund-raisers, or book parties, be very strict about how you use your time.

Vacations—Take Them

438 million. No, that's not the number of stars in the universe or sand dunes in the Sahara. 438 million is the estimated number of vacation days Americans failed to take in 2007. We were speechless, horrified, depressed just to learn it. How hard do we have to beg—TAKE A HOLIDAY!

Every year the travel gurus at Expedia.com conduct a survey on the benefits of vacation time (and yes, we get it, they have a dog in this fight—but even so, their findings are pretty compelling). Expedia cites both a peculiarly American puritanical work ethic—the fear of being seen as slackers—and the more prosaic tendency to horde vacation days for an unexpected emergency, as the main reasons behind this terrifying inability to take time off.

You get vacation for a reason. You need it. Take it. All of it. Then, if at all possible, take more. We don't need Expedia to tell us workers perform better if they've had a rest.

As you can see, we have pretty strong views on vacation. Everybody knows that Americans take a lot less vacation every year than the rest of the industrialized world, but did you know how much less?

Americans work two weeks longer than the work-till-you-drop Japanese and several weeks longer than most Europeans, where employees sometimes receive fifteen weeks of paid holiday per year. The United States is one of the very few industrialized nations where the government doesn't mandate any paid vacation days at all. And only Mexicans receive less paid vacation time than Americans—a pathetic six days a year. So just in case you were feeling guilty about booking your vacation time, don't. You probably aren't taking enough anyway.

You really do need it to recharge those flagging batteries. If it helps, see it like this: you are a more effective employee if you take your holiday, and since you get so little of it to start with, you better take it all to maximize your productivity when you are at work. But the reality is that in addition to working better, you will also think better and feel better. You will be a better mom, a better wife, and a better daughter and friend. And you will have the mental energy to really focus on something profound like Womenomics.

KATTY   A few years ago as I was set to go visit my family in Europe, an American colleague gasped: "You're really going for four weeks—wow, you Europeans take so much time off!" She's right, we are very lucky compared to most Americans. We can still, just, get away with taking month-long vacations. My colleague hadn't had more than a week's holiday in years—could never remember taking two weeks, let alone four. Suddenly, I felt like a slacker. My God—what would she make of my four-day workweek, my mental thirty-hour clock or my determination to be at home on the weekends? So I found myself slipping into the classic career machismo of pretending I was never off. Then it dawned on me—what I had done—which was basically achieve the same career status as that colleague but with far more time at home—was actually pretty impressive. I had managed professional satisfaction and perfectly respectable seniority without being wedded to my job. Surely—in today's crazy work-obsessed world—that was quite an accomplishment. It suggested that I had efficiently managed my time, performed well on the job, and knew my priorities, even though they went against the work-addicted norm. I never hide my holidays anymore, and in fact I get a certain pleasure from shocking people and telling them I'm off—yes, for a month.

We don't really understand why anyone needs help taking vacation time; neither of us ever seems to have enough. Whatever the reason, and we suspect some of it is that old office machismo we want you to get over right now, it is clear that some people never manage to use up their allotted days. So to make sure you don't sail into December with two weeks of unused leave in your pocket, here are a few tips on how to chill like a European.

- Plan your vacation early. We usually plan our next vacation the day after we return from vacation. If nothing else, it boosts morale!

- Put your vacation time in the office schedule months, not weeks, in advance. That way you're more likely to get the dates you want and everyone has plenty of warning time.

- If you're going away book your flights early; they cost less, and once you've paid for them you are less tempted to cancel the holiday.

- If you're not going away don't be tempted to offer to go into the office if they need you. This is still your vacation time, and even though you are at home you need to relax as much as possible. Remember those batteries!

- If you are staying home on holiday, unplug from technology as much as you would at the beach. If you have to check your e-mail account, leave the work ones unread. Turn off your cell phone. Cancel the newspapers. Take day trips to the countryside, where you'll be less tempted to waste time in front of the computer.

- Try taking a big chunk of time at once; if you usually take only one week, book two together. If you've already progressed to two, try three. You will be amazed at the difference. The more time you take at once, the more you really relax.

- Use a downturn to win more vacation time. If your company wants to reward you but can't give you a bonus, pay raise, or promotion because of falling profits, why not suggest an extra week's vacation as an alternative?

The time you can find by mining the concepts in this chapter, by herding those extra minutes and hours and days, will astound you. It's unclaimed and freely available—yours for the taking with a few smarter, not harder, tweaks to your system. And there's even more to reap, as you'll see in chapter 6, as you employ Womenomics wisdom toward some key strategic and psychological shifts that will put you firmly in control of your work life.

news you can use

1. Work smarter, and wield the 80–20 yardstick. Put out if it pays off.

2. Set meetings, deadlines, schedules early—and on your terms.

3. Exploit—but tame—your technology.

4. Take—and relish—all of your time off.

value added:
redefine your value,
value your time

There's no question that in the world of Womenomics, time is the critical new commodity. And to amass a meaningful amount of it, you're going to have to attempt more than just the starter steps we outlined in chapter 5. Think of it this way: as is the case with any other commodity, the less supply that's available, the greater the value. Certainly you know it's true for you personally. That's why, we're sure, you're reading this book

But it's also true in terms of the value of your time on the job. If you are constantly making room for every little assignment, your time will not seem particularly valuable. If something can be gotten on the cheap, it will remain cheap. But if you take control of your time and project an image of yourself as a person who will handle, let's say, only assignments at the highest levels, your time commodity value will skyrocket.

What does this mean? You will need to get much, much savvier about the way you work. You will learn in this chapter to take a leaf out of the old male playbook and start weighing every assignment, to choose the projects that really matter to the bosses. And as you nurture smart-time behavior you should also develop the bold and unashamed art of self-promotion. Image boosting, as we all know, isn't easy for women. But as you start to uncover, and luxuriate in, all the hours you will save, all of this will become second nature.

You Don't Have to Be Perfect

Somewhere buried deep in a woman's DNA is an insidious gene that makes us believe we are responsible for everything. Since our brains are wired to see and predict every possible scenario— every possible thing that could go wrong or could be better— it makes sense that we are driven in this direction. But this estrogen-fueled excess of diligence and responsibility can be a horrible waste of time.

You know what we mean. We worry not only about our jobs but about other people's tasks too. We organize birthday cakes and cards for colleagues, even when they might not want them. We fret about holiday gifts for assistants and teachers who'd be happy with something generic. We know all about it. We are just as guilty of compulsive perfectionism as you are.

KATTY   During the 2008 presidential elections I had to travel quite a bit for work. Before each trip I'd make sure the family was organized so that there was minimum disruption when I was gone. I'd see that the fridge was full, meals planned, the babysitter organized for the extra hours, and the children set up with playdates. My husband, Tom, didn't ask me to fix stuff, I just did it automatically. Then I found I was getting overstretched, and the travel was tiring anyway without all that domestic organizing and worrying. It began to occur to me that Tom never felt he should check the contents of the fridge before he went on a work trip. Soon I was getting resentful. Where was the recognition for all this stress and time I put in to make sure the house ran smoothly in my absence? But really it was all my own fault. Tom certainly never asked me to do all that shopping and planning before I left. He is a very involved, capable parent who is quite up to the task of running the house by himself for a few days. No, I was micromanaging—big time. So when planning the next trip, I decided just to pack my own bag and go. And guess what? Everyone was just fine (OK, so I did come back and find ten pounds of cod in the freezer because my husband's grasp of cooking portions was a little undeveloped but, hey, that's not the end of the world.) Nobody starved (there was plenty of fish), my husband arranged for the babysitter, and the kids got to school on time. Without me! Amazing! Of course a part of me, control freak that I am, was a bit put out—the universe of my home clearly doesn't depend entirely on me and me alone! But once I'd dealt with my domestic ego, I found it was also very liberating.

When it comes to the work environment, our determination to control every detail of a project is just as pronounced as it is in the kitchen or playroom. For professional, ambitious women, this trait is even more acute—we tend to be overachieving perfectionists, so of course we don't trust anyone else to do things right. After all, we know best!

CLAIRE   I used to be a maniacal perfectionist, especially at work. I felt that every piece I put on the air had to have the same amount of blood, sweat, and tears poured into it. I'd labor into the night making endless changes, and often ruining the evenings of coworkers and friends and my spouse. I've finally realized that such perfectionism is not an option anymore if I want to see my family and keep colleagues happy. And so I've adjusted. I've figured out when I can do a "good" job and when I need to do a "perfect" job. With almost every assignment I get or propose, I make a decision at the start about how much time it deserves, before I start my "perfectionizing." Basically, I've learned to be comfortable being "good enough" when it makes sense.

Here are two key lifestyle changes for all of you hyper-control-freak perfectionists out there: first, think "good enough"; second, start delegating.

Good Enough

By "good enough" we mean absolutely, definitely, *not* our very best, *not* perfect. We are actively encouraging you to perform occasionally below standard. Go on, you have our permission. In fact we suggest a trial period where you make a conscious habit of NOT doing things as well as you usually do—and even then we bet you'll still be good and not just mediocre. It's a radical concept, but once you get the hang of it, you'll be liberated to focus on high-value/high-return activities in your professional and personal life.

"You have to remember," counsels Julie Wellner, an architect from Kansas City, "are you trying to be good enough in your own eyes or everybody else's eyes?" Julie has set up her own firm and created a work enviroment where she can be with her children when she chooses. But she still fights the lure of perfectionism. "That's where we fall short compared to men. Men are better at saying, 'OK, this is good enough in my eyes.' Women are constantly saying, 'Is this good enough in the world's eyes?' "

Once you've mastered the ability of being able to use "good enough" strategically, you'll be able to shift your performance up a gear and be "totally excellent" when it really counts. After all there's no way you can have time to do everything to your highest standards all the time. Remember, that's the road to sixty-hour workweeks—the road we are trying to destroy. No, if you want a sane life, permanent perfection is just not possible. Get over it! We are not looking to be judged "good enough" by Gandhi.

Embracing "good enough" is simply a smart power move. Think of it this way: we're so good and so in demand we can't possibly do everything to perfection. And, by the way, our "good enough" is great.

Letting Go

The most successful people—the Big Picture Thinkers—don't try to do everything. Instead, they hand things off. It's better for them, better for their boss, and it's better for their company too because it allows younger talent to flourish.

As the boss of her own communications company, Christine Heenan *had* to learn the art of delegation. For her it has meant a deliberate process of keeping her perfectionist tendencies in check. She hated to let go of anything, because she knew just how she wanted it done, and after all, can't the boss always do it best? But if she wanted time with her two boys as well then there simply wasn't enough of her to go around.

"I think successful delegating means empowering people other than you to do something maybe not exactly as you would do it, but to do it instead of you," she explains. "I might say, 'This press release is not written the way I would have written it.' But it's gone out, and I see an e-mail back from the client saying it sounds fine, and I've just got to leave it at that."

She faces the same issues at home. "Say my sitter has allowed my son Colin to do his homework over at his friend Ben's house," Christine says. "I think he should do his homework at home before he goes to Ben's, but she's there and she's in charge and once you know no one is hurt and no one is in trouble, then you just have to let it go."

Delegating also sends a cunning reminder to your bosses, babysitters, and husband that you are too busy to do everything. It can be another form of saying "no" that leaves everyone better off.

Remember Lauren Tyler, our private equity banker in New York, who balances three children and two stepchildren with a determination to maintain work-life control in a world where there usually isn't any? She says delegating is the key to her ability to stay in a job she loves and have time for the family she also loves. "It solves three problems for me—it leaves me in the clear to get my job done, gives someone below me an opportunity to shine, and it builds loyalty. It all comes back to help me and the organization. But you do have to let go!"

That is often easier said than done. Accepting that some delegated tasks may not be done precisely to your exacting standards can cause stress. How do successful women manage this tricky terrain?

Here are some delegating tips:

1. If you are overstretched, but a delegating novice, choose one task to delegate and then delegate it right away, before you have second thoughts. As you grow more comfortable, use the 80–20 Rule to figure out which tasks can be handed off.

2. Ask who is right for the job. It does not always have to be the team star. Someone new and keen may be perfect for some tasks. Someone with more experience may be better for others.

3. Once you've chosen the person, explain the task, the time frame, and the review process. Make yourself available for specific questions but don't check up on their progress every ten minutes. Remember you have delegated to win time—not to spend it checking up on the delegatee!

4. Ask yourself: is there something here for me to learn in doing this task? Will it provide me with new skills and competence that will be useful in the future, or is it a routine task that I could do quickly—but that won't necessarily add to my value as an employee? And could it present a learning opportunity for one of my junior staffers? What's routine for you may be a learning opportunity for others. Those are the perfect tasks to delegate.

5. Enlist your executive assistant, if you're lucky enough to have one, in the cause. Anybody who can help you by fielding phone calls, deciding what decisions can be postponed if it's your day off, or even cunningly pulling you out of meetings that you didn't want to sit through until the bitter end, is an invaluable asset. Treat assistants well and with respect, it goes without saying, but don't hesitate to ask them to work for you. Your assistant is not your friend. She, or, yes, even he, is your bodyguard.

Miriam Decker, a top Wall Street investor, asked us to change her name because of the cutthroat nature of her business. "I just heard one male partner here remarking that anybody on the 6:30 P.M. train home doesn't deserve to be at the firm," she says, laughing and grimacing at the same time. "You can't even risk putting an 'out-of-the-office' automatic e-mail reply on your e-mail account," she continues, "Bad form." Miriam says an assistant is one of the keys to keeping her life livable, and somewhat under wraps. "With a good assistant," she explains, "I can make my life work. They know the kids, the schools, when to interrupt a meeting for a phone call, how to mention I'm at 'a breakfast' when I'm in late. I learned from my partner's assistant. One day I asked where he was. 'At breakfast,' she told me. Then two hours later when he came in I went into his office to talk and he said, 'I just had the best workout!' I laughed to myself and was reminded that this is nothing new. Men have been doing it for years."

Promote Thyself

Would it make sense to give away Nobel Prizes anonymously? Are Pulitzer winners kept under wraps? Do CEOs who navigate a successful merger hide the fact? No, of course not. And for good reason. The world likes winners

And self-promotion is a basic part of business life. Informing others of a success is just as much about keeping them in the loop as is informing them about a failure. Working smart time requires that you get the most bang for your professional buck, which means that when you score a win, you need to let the right people know. And remember—your boss wants to revel in your victory.

As with everything else in life, there's a right way and a wrong way to do this. The wrong way is fairly obvious (gloating to your own staff, babbling incessantly about a win, giving yourself obnoxious shiny stars and smiley faces). The right way is not so obvious, but it's extremely important. In our experience, women shy away from this kind of self-promotion. *Don't.*

Just one example of what the real cost to women is when they don't sell themselves: a 2002 study that looked at the starting salaries of men and women graduating from Carnegie Mellon with master's degrees found that only 7 percent of the women negotiated for more money, compared to 57 percent of the men. On average, those men got an extra four thousand dollars.

The following tips will keep you within the lines of intelligently informing the command chain about your successes, without falling into useless, time-wasting, animosity-inspiring bragging.

1. Try for an informative, casual, but straightforward tone. **You say:** "Bob, did you hear? We nailed that Backstra account. It was a thrill to run that closing! Thanks for the opportunity." **They hear:** You're just so jazzed about the victory you couldn't keep it in.

Robin Ehlers says she used to be shy about calling attention to her work, but over time she's realized higher-ups actually appreciate it, and they view it as part of her loyalty to the company. "People that I work for know that I love this company, I love what I do, I'm always reliable," she explains. "So the way I get my name out there, is that, when I do something well, I always copy my boss."

2. Don't simply rattle off a list of accomplishments. It's much better to handle references to a recent success in a conversation. Often it can include you asking lots of questions, and even offering praise. **You say:** "How are things going on the Canada account?" . . . "Ah, yes, I had a sense when I finally got them to agree to that concession last week that they'd eventually sign on.

It was tough going though. They were really dug in. Oh, and thanks for that idea about throwing in the regional business. When I finally dangled that, they agreed. Congratulations, Bob. It's just great news for the company." **They think:** I clearly have a brilliant employee who is learning from me.

3. Be self-deprecating. **You say:** "I'll never forget that moment last month when I got the All-America service award . . . and I tripped on my way up to the stage!" **They hear:** You're clearly a star but have a great sense of humor about it.

4. See yourself as others may see you. This is crucial to managing your image. The way you are perceived inside the company may not be fair, but it is what it is, and if you are working there, you have to deal with it. That can be why, says Melissa James, self-promotion or powerful talk from women can make us seem like that *B* word we all hate so much. "Sometimes I know I intimidate men," she concedes. Not fair, but since she's self-aware, she can calibrate. **You say:** "Ted, we couldn't have closed the deal without your advice on the product numbers." **They think:** A well-mannered, perceptive employee—she's a winner.

5. Tell a story. These can work really well and are easy and entertaining to pull out of your hat when you come face-to-face with higher-ups. If you think hard enough, you can find drama in any recent success.

You say: "Jim—what a wild trip to Minneapolis that was. The plane landed four hours late . . . and when we got off . . . our bags hadn't made the flight, including our PowerPoint presentation! Well—you can imagine my team was demoralized. Luckily, I'd been rehearsing the presentation for a week—and our whole team knew it cold. I rallied them . . . told them wrinkled clothes and no gadgets didn't matter, that we were selling ourselves. And the client was bowled over. I've never felt so proud of our people."

They hear: You are clearly a stellar team leader who isn't afraid to talk about bad moments, who motivates her people, can pull the company out of a jam, and most important, seems to thrive on the experience!

By the way, Melissa James, who thinks all women have a hard time with the promotion business, thinks praising the team is always the best way to go.

"Every time I have an opportunity to talk about my team I send an e-mail up the chain. That's the whole point really, of being a leader. Motivating and supporting others."

The Strategic Yes

A key nexus of working smarter not harder and being a savvy self-promoter is to focus on the high-profile assignments that your boss really cares about. That's how you get the biggest bang. And in learning to recognize those moments, you will come to see that occasionally there are assignments that might threaten to wreak havoc with your schedule, but they might also provide you with a huge payoff. When the two of us give each other advice, we've taken to calling them Strategic Yes moments. These are the times when you need to realize how much mileage you will get out of saying yes. These are the times when it might cost you personally but it will pay off so well professionally that it's worth that super early start, the Sunday in the office, that tedious trip to Houston. You need to keep an eye out for these opportunities and bank them, so you can coast later.

Here's how:

1. Know Your Boss

Beyond your own job description, make it your business to be on top of your boss's pet issues—if it's his priority, make it your priority. Don't bust a gut on something he's not very interested in. But if he has a client, concern, or commodity he is keen on, you will get a lot of mileage by performing well, and putting in the extra hours, in those areas.

For Stephanie Hampton at Marriott the Strategic Yes moment came on an environmental project that she knew was very important to her boss. Marriott was planning to invest $2 million to protect the Amazon rain forest—and it needed a major communications rollout. This green initiative was personally sponsored by the company's CFO and Stephanie's EVP, so it had high-level backing.

"It was game-changing and the first-of-its-kind for the industry, so I felt like I was part of that. And I felt like if I did my job, we could help win the hearts and minds of many customers, investors, and employees through this very real initiative to address climate change. I had to work some late nights and a weekend or two, but it wasn't systemic, so I was happy to do it."

2. Keep Tabs on Company/Industry Buzz

This is similar to knowing your boss. You have to put a bit of extra effort in, but there are opportunities to score high here. If you can keep an eye on the current hot issues either in your company, or even more broadly within your industry, you can direct your energy into those high-profile, high-reward projects that are grabbing everyone's attention. And if you are ahead of the curve on buzz, it also gives you a chance to leap on those areas early on and claim them as yours. It makes you and your boss look good, which helps everyone.

In our industry that means being aware of the new story lines that editors are fixated on—in yours it could be the implementation of a new technology, the effect of a new legal precedent, a hot new vein of medical research, or how to channel concerns about the energy crisis into profits for your company. Whatever it is, keep your ears and eyes open and make company news by being a trend leader.

3. Make Yourself Essential

Melissa James of Morgan Stanley says that especially when the economy is in a downturn, it's critical to develop this skill. Assess what you do that nobody else can do, and that your boss could not handle without you. And if you're not coming up with anything, focus on this fast. "But none of this is easy," notes James. "It can be complicated to figure out exactly what is the best use of your time for your bosses and for you. It takes some intuition." It also takes good communication. Don't hesitate to check in with your superior frequently to go over priorities, yours and hers. Over time, you'll see how you should best direct your energies.

4. Strategic Yeses to Make Up for Lots of Nos!

Both of us are constantly tallying our quotas of nos and yeses. It's a question of balance. If we've turned down a run of assignments, trips, or stories we realize it may be a good time to say yes to a project. And if you want to get extra kudos, offer to take something on before you're even asked. Make sure that yes is heard loud and clear for maximum professional capital (which of course you can spend later to win yourself time).

If you are generally allergic to taking on extra assignments, this may not come easily—so keep your female sixth sense on your boss's expectations. If you pick up hints that you've seemed to be underperforming/slacking off/not quite a team player in recent weeks—throw out a keen, confident yes and knuckle under for a short burst.

And, a confession, we don't always get this right ourselves!

CLAIRE I'd been on the road for work every week for three weeks back to back. Moreover, I had a trip to Italy coming up for *Good Morning America* that I was dreading, since I'd been gone so much. At the same time, I'd also been getting pressure to travel to Texas to cover Jenna Bush's wedding just three days after the Italy trip. My husband and I wanted to have our daughter's birthday party that weekend, so between that and all the travel I decided to say no to covering the Bush wedding. I thought that was the end of it. Hardly. I got a call from an executive explaining that the execs felt I should go, and that everyone thought I had "enough" time between my trips to justify it.

For some reason that just made my blood boil. I called the female executive who was making this decision and coldly explained why I would not be going. She countered, saying that the network was assigning me and, again, I had "enough time" between trips. I exploded, questioning why they could make that judgment about my family life, reminding her I was not a "serf" (yes, I said that) to be dispatched at will, and throwing out all sorts of other things including hysterical tears. I ended by saying I was not going, and if that meant I'd be fired then so be it. (I happened to be writing *Womenomics* at the time, and I think all of the focus on empowerment was making me giddy).

Since Katty was in the middle of an interview, I called my husband immediately. Maybe he was thinking about our bank balance, but he encouraged me to take a step back. He suggested that we celebrate Della's birthday the next weekend and that he'd be around for the kids if I had to go. Most importantly, he pointed out that this sounded like a high-profile assignment from the network's point of view, and one that would get me a lot of airtime on a lot of shows all in one swoop. I hadn't seen the big picture like that. It took me a few hours to recover, but I called back later and told the executive I could in fact go. She was quite cheerful and grateful, and acted like my emotional outburst was no big deal. Phew.

Anyhow, I realized later than I should have seen that the trip to Texas was clearly an opportunity. And in fact it turned out to be. Three days in Texas, and I was on every broadcast. Now, maybe I was able to make an important point with my approach, and still get the benefit, but I'm not sure I'd suggest that as a strategy. Too draining. Especially for my husband!

Strategic Nos

We can guarantee with absolute certainty that there will come a time in your professional life when, however savvy you are about rejecting perfection in favor of "good enough," about delegating, self-promoting, and delivering those strategic yeses, you will have no choice but to assert yourself with a big, definitive *NO*. It can be career changing. We're talking about Alpha stuff here. You've been offered partner but just can't accept and stay sane. The Tokyo office is yours, but you know it won't work with your life. That EVP slot is on the table, if you'll bust your gut and marriage for it.

This is the time to know when and how to kick Womenomics into top gear in order to turn down a major commitment, without driving your career into a brick wall.

These are tough. They are often moments of real confrontation. They may involve an intractable boss, an unfair but critical assignment, perhaps turning down a promotion. They can be terrifying to imagine. And that terror can keep you from sticking up for yourself, from setting reasonable boundaries, from getting what you want.

It might reassure you to learn that even seemingly apocalyptic, ugly nos can have very good outcomes. And even when they don't, the players survive. We know, we've both done it.

KATTY   It started with an innocent phone call from my agent. Would I be interested in talking to a major US network about a job as White House correspondent? Sure I was happy to talk; I mean this was a big deal. No American network had ever had a Brit reporting from the White House before. And yes, I was flattered. The meeting went well, I liked the people, they must have liked me—I was offered the job. The agent was thrilled and pushed hard— "You have to take this, it's a major step up in your career here, if you don't I'm not quite sure what you do want." But I was already having doubts. The BBC is a public broadcaster that doesn't pay well, but it did give me a lot of freedom and a lot of time off. I knew I'd never get that kind of control over my schedule at a U.S. network. My vacation would be cut in half, I'd have to be at the White House every day, and on call whenever needed. These are tough, competitive organizations, and I'd be a newcomer, and a foreigner to boot, with a lot to prove. I felt under pressure to say yes—from the network, which kept calling, from my agent, who was growing increasingly exasperated, and from my own susceptible ego. But in the end I went with my gut—the idea of that job made me miserable, so what was the point of taking it? I said "no" and had to say it again, several times with increasing firmness. Luckily, I had Claire to advise me!

CLAIRE I felt something in my stomach, but I couldn't identify it exactly. Surely it must be butterflies. There was a new anchoring gig at our network, and I was a front-runner! Just a few years ago I would have done armed combat for a job opportunity like that. And there was no mistaking the thrill that my agent, my friends, and relatives were getting from the prospect. But as the days went on, I realized that the feeling in my stomach wasn't butterflies, it was dread. Did I really want to uproot my family from Washington to New York? After years of feeling I was in a backwater, I'd grown to love the more relaxed lifestyle of the nation's capital. And it was not the ideal time in my husband's career to make a move either. My agent suggested I could commute to New York. Maybe. After all, how could I really say no to an anchoring job if it were offered? That's supposed to be the pinnacle of our business—something we all strive to do. And network executives were whispering in my ear about how much they hoped I'd say yes. "We need someone like you in that chair," said one at a dinner gathering. They need me! It was the most seductive of siren calls. But all I could think about was whether I really wanted to take on the responsibility and the long hours. I had a young child and another on the way, and finally felt I'd achieved a routine that was working in my life. After weeks of agonizing, I realized I couldn't do what the company might need and also be my best version of a mother. Some people can, but I couldn't. The day before I was supposed to fly to New York to check my "chemistry" with a male anchor, I told my agent to pull me out of the running. Strategically, I decided to focus not only on lifestyle but also on the fact that I loved the job I was doing, which was true. The executives were startled, to say the least. Did it close some doors for me? Probably. I'm not anchoring as much as I once was, for example. But in the long run, I've come to believe that my willingness to say "no" didn't really damage my standing at the company. In fact, it was probably best for everybody. It's kept me doing what I really love to do, which is write and report. It also let me make a statement about priorities, which was healthy for me and ABC.

Even when strategic nos are not as career changing as rejecting a seemingly glittering promotion, they are still remarkably stressful. Sometimes it's a question of standing your ground against a single unreasonable request or particularly belligerent boss.

Every Wednesday Miriam Decker's big boss holds a small staff meeting with about twenty people, but one Wednesday Miriam knew she'd need to work from home. "I had two important school meetings and two doctor's appointments," she says. "I just had too much I needed to squeeze in, and I don't live near the office." She could see tension coming when she heard that her partner and supervisor wouldn't be able to attend that Wednesday meeting either, and their golden rule was that one of them always went. She decided to break that rule and go ahead with her plans anyway. She ignored the stress building in her mind and told her partner she'd handle the meeting by conference call from home. She didn't tell him why. "I could tell he was bothered when I told him," she says, "and I did feel guilty for a few minutes." But she didn't offer to change her schedule.

How did she get the guts to stand her ground? "I thought about the fact that there are fifty-two of those high-level meetings in a year, and I'm missing one." And she moved on.

Christy Runninghan will never forget the down-and-dirty confrontation with her unreconstructed boss at Best Buy a few years ago. She was supposed to be able to leave work early on

Fridays in the summer, but he didn't want to let her out the door if he was still there.

"I'm not somebody who confronts my boss or something like that you know. . . . I grew up in Catholic school for goodness sakes, that whole Catholic guilt is kind of going along with what you're supposed to be doing," she remembers, laughing now. "I finally had to say, 'Look, I am documenting all of these hours, you want me to stay here until five-thirty or six like you? But I also have to be in here at seven o'clock to fulfill my duties. Look at how many hours that would be."

He was tough, and unsympathetic, she remembers, but she'd prepared her argument well and was able to make her case. "And I said, 'And here's what I'm taking for lunch, so this is well over what I should be working in a work week, and I'm not going to be staying until five-thirty or six o'clock. Just because you are coming in later and staying later, doesn't mean I have to do the same thing. Here's what I'm doing, and I'm still fulfilling my job requirements in more than enough hours to do the job.' " He was not happy, but she got to leave early on Fridays.

Not all bosses will react well to Strategic Nos, so choose your battles. But take heart as you explore this unfamiliar landscape. There are savvy bosses out there who get it.

"I do remember for a long time not ever wanting to say, 'I'm home with a sick child today.' " Julie Wellner, who owns that architecture firm in Kansas City, says she struggled with being open about her scheduling needs, and as a boss, she was also leery of her employees being open about their personal lives, even though she granted flexibility. Now she sees that honesty works, within limits.

"Now I don't mind anybody in the office saying 'I can't do that, I'm gonna be at a baseball game.' As long as it is straightforward and doesn't become too much information. In other words, if you say, if I or one of my staff says, 'I'm not going to be there because I have to attend something at my child's school,' I think that's just fine. What I don't want them to say is, 'My mom is sick and I'm gonna have to help my sister move and blah blah blah.'"

"I think honestly, if you're doing your job you don't need to be there twelve hours a day. It's an unrealistic thing and it's an unhappy thing and it doesn't work in the long run," says Geraldine Laybourne. "You shouldn't have to work that many hours. You're not productive, you can't be coming up with good ideas."

And remember this key Womenomics fact as you contemplate whether you can turn something down or leave the office: a good manager, who is truly looking for results, will see through meaningless face-time.

"A lot of these people are just running in place. A lot of it is, how can I put the face-time in so the boss thinks I'm really great?" says Laybourne, shaking her head. "That is a needy needy needy kind of thing. I think people need to understand themselves, what they bring to the party. Think hard, be fresh for thinking, and stick to their guns."

This may seem to go without saying, but we'd better say it, and probably more than once: you have to be a good performer to pull this off. Setting limits, saying no, being lazy like a fox—it only works out if you're cunning like a fox as well. After all, no boss is going to offer you bonuses and promotions simply because you're less available. But every boss will offer incentives if you happen to be less available but are also accomplishing better, higher-caliber, higher-impact assignments without hiccups or delays. Every boss we've talked with, and every woman we've interviewed with a flexible schedule, says the same thing. It works best if they really like you; and indeed the flexibility itself often makes them like you more because you perform better.

Don't Ask. Don't Tell.

When you put all these separate strategies and techniques together you may find that you can actually create a flexible schedule on your own—without even asking permission, negotiating a new deal, or, most critically, taking a pay cut. Let's face it—some companies just aren't prone to offering you the possibility formally. It will be up to you to make it happen. Lauren, for example, says it's unusual to get a formal flexibility agreement in her line of work.

"In investment banking or private equity it's tough to do, probably because, even these days, there's so much money at stake," she explains. "It's just the culture. The group norm is to work as hard as you can."

Miriam goes one step further. "You'll always have younger men or younger women ready to steal your lunch money, as we call it. If you don't work your tail off, you probably won't be wanted as part of the group. So if you want flexibility, don't ask about it, just take it," she advises. "It's basically don't ask, don't tell."

Most of us are not in industries quite that cutthroat, but we still may need to create our own utopia. So together with all of the savvy techniques we've laid out, here's a path to follow that will let you start to set precedents, create routines, and carve out a way of working that will leave some colleagues wondering, "How did she get this great work setup?" But once it is set in place, your new schedule will be hard to roll back.

- Make a point of leaving the office a few times during the day for "meetings." Let everyone know you'll be on your BlackBerry. While you are gone, send several e-mails back to the office dealing with pressing issues immediately. People will start to realize you don't need to be there to be on top of things.

- Come in at 7 A.M. one morning. Make sure you boss knows how early you were there. Be superefficient in a public way throughout the day, meet deadlines, take on new projects. But at lunchtime, announce you have an appointment at 3 P.M. Try to have an assignment finished or some other impressive piece of work done that you can hand off as you head out. (Don't apologize and don't promise to be up all night.)

- Or stay late one evening, and again, make sure people know. As your colleagues leave the office, let them know you'll be working from home the next morning, since you want to get a jump start on the day and avoid the commute. While you are working at home, send a slew of e-mails and information to all concerned. Let them *feel* you work.

- Pick a project that is not due for a while. Get most of it done in advance but don't tell your boss. Then let him know that since you're an early bird, you'd like to get a "head start" on the project from home at 6 A.M. the next day. Put it on his desk when you walk in the door at noon. Highly impressive! He'll think you did it all that day from home and wonder whether working from home is more productive!

Tim Ferriss in *The 4-Hour Workweek* has some quite creative suggestions about becoming "ill" but insisting to your employer that you can handle your work at home, and then while at home, you suddenly become so productive both you and your boss realize you may be on to a good thing in terms of efficiency and productivity! We love the chutzpah of this one.

So you get the idea. Start small, but be assumptive. Always have your work covered in spades, so that nobody can say you are not getting everything done. If you can find ways to prove that you are somehow superefficient even though you are at the office less, then all the better. Soon you will find that your quirky schedule is simply accepted, and nobody will question when you are in or out because they know your work gets done on time. Once that happens, all you need is a few more tips to keep things running smoothly.

- Go public with deadlines. Announce your internal limits out loud to whomever listens in a way that is focused on productivity. "Gang, let's get moving on this. I'm out of here at 4 P.M." "Guys, let's spend the morning on this. I'm not around this afternoon." "We've got to finish the Braden proposal by Friday. I'm away next week." It will make you seem efficient, bottom-line oriented, and will help to ingrain the notion that your schedule will not change.

- Energy executive Sarah Slusser says being clear about schedules and time limits is both good common sense and helpfully respectful—two things that in the end make you look strong. "A lot of work is teamwork, so you can't just disappear," she says. "You have to let people know ahead of time what you're doing. That really helps. If you let people know you need a flexible schedule and tell them exactly what it is, colleagues know to build around that, and they think you've done the responsible thing by informing them. It's a hard thing to do, though; you feel like you're weak by saying I want to leave work early on Fridays. But it's not weak; you have another obligation or another responsibility or another priority, and that's who you are."

- Be assertive and clear about your schedule, and depending on the company, don't hide the family. Most places have moved beyond the Stone Age. Once you have a pattern established, the more truth the better. "Can I take that home with me? I'll have it reviewed tonight. I've got soccer to coach at 4 P.M."

- Offer alternatives. Christy Runningen at Best Buy says having that attitude breeds understanding and agreement. "I've finally gotten to the point where most of the time I can just say 'I won't be available here,'" she explains, "but I try to be up front and also say, 'I can do this, or would this work instead?'"

Exceptions

There are of course professions that absolutely require your physical presence at specific times. It's not possible to get a knee operation from a surgeon who's out playing with her children in the park. In these cases, being cunning doesn't immediately pay off in terms of time away from the office, but it can bring other benefits that lead to the same effect. If you perform well, over time you will be in a much stronger position to renegotiate your whole deal—to define your job in the terms and times you want.

Linda Brooks, our New York lawyer, whose law firm operates, like most law firms, on billable hours, says her profession does not really encourage time-saving techniques.

"You're not going to see a lot of people spending a lot of time figuring out how to bill fewer hours," she concedes. "Even if you get your work done much faster, the partners will still want you to be billing, or working, a certain amount of hours. I think the work-smart model, just fundamentally and economically, it's kind of at odds with the billable hour," she says. Obviously if you work smarter and more efficiently you will be seen as a better employee—you just might not get to take your reward in "downtime." But, one could argue, Linda's smart, effective work is the reason her partners were open to her taking a pay cut and taking a day off a week. "I think by making this decision," she adds, "I am by definition working smarter. I just try to get as much done in the four days that I am in the office as I can so it frees up more time on Friday."

Economically, it wasn't the best thing for her. But psychologically, it's given her the life she wants, and she was more than willing to pay the price, literally, for that freedom.

Dear Gens X and Y

KATTY   I was twenty-nine years old and living in Tokyo as a foreign correspondent for the BBC when I found out I was pregnant with my first child. I phoned up my best friend, a colleague from work, and burst into tears. "I don't know if I want kids. What about my career? No one will ever take me seriously again." For the first time in my life I was really loving my work, getting praise from my bosses and self-esteem from my rising profile. If I left work at 8 P.M. I felt I was going home early. I was convinced that having a baby would mean the end of all that. I'd be put on the "mommy track." Thirteen years and four children later I realize that's not true. My career has gone through various permutations, some fast-track, some slow, but it does still exist. I do know, however, that I have benefited, as I've sought flexibility over the years, from my early days of hard work, and from the career base I established for myself in my hard-charging twenties.

Women who are just starting out these days are well ahead of where we were twenty years ago. It never occurred to us to think ahead about children—we'd chugged back the corporate Kool-Aid. The confrontation with reality came hard. But today's young women are different. They are already planning long term and asking balance questions right from the start. Gens X and Y, you are smarter than we were, and you're right, it is never too soon to build healthy work habits.

But the reality is that you may not be able to walk into a company for your first job and demand significant flexibility. So in the early part of your career, you may well have to make sacrifices, adopt the dragon-slayer attitude, and pretend that you are dying to do nothing more than pull four all-nighters in a row.

Valerie Jarrett, President Barack Obama's senior adviser and a family friend, says she's worked hard to help her daughter, Laura, who is in law school, navigate the new work terrain. A lawyer herself who was running the Habitat Company in Chicago until last year, she tells her daughter to choose her profession carefully so she can have a life and a family.

"There are so many more options now for women, but you still have to be savvy about your choices, and know what the profession will demand," she says.

Jarrett says she also encourages her daughter to do the hard work early, so that she will have earned the flexibility she needs, when she needs it.

"We had long conversations about goodwill. I told her, 'Laura, this is what gets you through life, and you do want to build it up.' So, for example, in the beginning of the summer she worked like a dog. I said there's only one chance to make a first good impression, and so you've got to work exceptionally hard at the beginning if you want people to see what you're made of basically."

"I tell women, build up that goodwill bank, make those sacrifices early," says Melissa James of Morgan Stanley. "It only gets

harder over the course of your career to make those time sacrifices, and if you build up that goodwill bank, hopefully you'll be
able, at some later stage, to cash in on it."

That said, you can still learn much from the techniques already discussed in chapters 3, 4, and 5. You should already be
thinking big and using your time well. And we definitely don't
want you to become a doormat—work hard, but keep focused on
your life-work priorities. Be certain that the projects you are
spending time on will pay off for you. Don't let yourself get handed
all the drudge work. These are invaluable skills and will show
from the start that you are leadership material. Start experimenting with our techniques now, when the stakes are not so high.

Thirty-two-year-old Anne Hurst, who has a master's degree
in public policy, just quit one nonprofit job as an educational
consultant to move to another called Jump Start. She took
a $10,000 or 20 percent annual pay cut to do it. Why? Like so
many young women of her and perhaps your generation, work-
life balance is already important to her.

"There was very little respect for the fact that I had needs and
desires outside of work, the fact that I wanted to go to the gym or
go running. Of course everyone would say it was fine, but in reality, the number of hours that I worked, the office situation that I
was in, really didn't respect making me a happy person."

Anne is about to get married and wants to have children, so
working for a company that would offer flexibility is already very
much on her mind.

"I definitely thought about it when I was thinking about
taking this job. I thought about the atmosphere in the office and
how I would feel more relaxed if I have a kid, about my needs to
adjust my schedule from time to time. My last job had horrible
deadlines. You had to work through no matter what, which is
completely not acceptable if you have to go home and get your
kid from day care."

It's also important that you carefully study the industry where you are working or considering working. Do your research. Zero in on its track record with women. Is there a large percentage of women in the workforce? In management? Those would obviously be good signs. And what kinds of lives do those women lead? Talk to some of the women there about their experience in that business. Before you launch yourself on a certain path, ask if it's an industry where it's easier for women to pull off the New All.

Maybe you don't have children at home, and maybe you aren't thinking about having any yet, or even at all. Maybe you really do want to dedicate most of your free time to your career. Even then you will benefit from honing your skills at buying time, and being more efficient and ridding yourself of guilt.

And when you've earned a few years or decades of corporate credit and want to cash them in to buy more freedom because smart time isn't enough, we've got the ultimate guide to negotiating a whole new deal. Just ahead you'll find our road map to more formal flexibility and an entirely new life.

news you can use

1. If you try to be perfect all of the time, you will work all of the time.

2. Be savvy—delegate, self-promote, and learn when to say no, and yes, strategically.

3. Note to Gens X and Y—like your mothers said, you are never too young to adopt healthy habits.

nine rules to negotiate nirvana: how to change your whole work deal

O n Sunday as the day wore on," remembers Christy Runningen, "I would become more unhappy, more cranky and more frantic."

Oh, that Sunday evening feeling. It's a state of mind we can relate to.

"You know that gross feeling you get in your stomach," Christy explains, "before the workweek starts, thinking, 'OK, now I'm going to be locked in, I'm going to be at the office, for these forty-plus hours.'"

How about a world where you never have that Sunday evening feeling? Where that nausea in the pit of your stomach is banished?

How about a world where even the concept of eight to five-thirty for forty-nine weeks a year doesn't exist at all? A world where you can work when you want, where you want, how you want—as long as you get the job done and done well.

How about a world where you never have to swallow the panic

as you add up the waking hours you have out of the office and realize you just aren't spending enough time with your children? A world where you don't feel like crying once a week because you're overstretched, underappreciated, and flat out at the end of your tether?

We are talking about a world where Monday morning feels (almost) like Friday afternoon. Where going to the office is no longer a depressing duty but a chosen pleasure. Where work is rewarding but not regimented.

That's our nirvana. It can be yours too. You *can* change the whole structure of your work life—toss the whole thing up in the air and let it fall in a pattern of your choosing. Women all around the country are doing it. Many more than you think. In this chapter we will show you how to go beyond playing with the margins to squeeze minutes or hours out of your day. You will learn how to renegotiate the whole deal. We will teach you to think big and bold, and we will show you how other women have gone about getting a New All.

Oh, and by the way, we'll show you how to make your bosses love nirvana too!

How to Change *Your* Deal

There are literally hundreds of different ways you can shape the work deal you want. Remember Stephanie Hampton? She's our public relations whiz at Marriott hotels. After years as a full-on workaholic, she's now scaled back to a four-day week. Guess how she got her four-day week? She asked! It took her a ridiculously long time to do it though.

"I was on maternity leave with my son and I just knew I didn't want to go back to work full time. I talked it over with my husband, and we agreed I'd ask for a four-day week. The only problem was, I couldn't summon up the courage to ask. Every day my friends and family said, 'So have you asked yet?' Eventually my mom came over and pushed me, and when I finally did, my boss was surprisingly accommodating."

In fact Stephanie got her new deal fairly easily—once she actually made the request. Her boss wasn't freaked-out, didn't fire her, demote her, or send her to "mommy track" purgatory. She is still a high-powered, well-valued, top-performing member of Marriott's management team. Indeed Stephanie suspects he was expecting the call. But, wow, what a lot of stress to get there.

Do you know the number one reason women don't get the New All they want at work? They don't ask for it. One day we won't have to make our individual pitches; the world really is changing, and before very long all companies will realize the benefits of flexibility. But until they do, you have to ask.

We don't know a boss who will casually saunter up to your desk and suggest, "Clara, you seem a bit overstretched these days. I bet it's tricky balancing all the different parts of your life. But we really want to keep you here and want to make you happy. Wouldn't you feel saner if we just adjusted your schedule? Why don't I just rely on you to get the work done and you can do it from wherever you like, whenever you like? How does that sound?"

Dream on. (OK, if anybody does know bosses like this out there, we want to track them down for our best-bosses listing. Send names to our Web site.)

Listen, we sympathize. We know it's hard to confront your boss and ask for something "extra," and it is somehow particularly hard for women. The thought of marching into the corner office and asking for a better schedule brings out a feeling of dread. Suddenly we're ten years old, not thirty-five. The boss has morphed into our meanest teacher ever and we're back in school-rules panic mode all over again. The knot in our stomach gets tighter, and we find excuses not to pick up the phone, request the meeting and make the case. But you've been through the Womenomics training circuit now and have banished all of those unconfident thoughts from your head, so you have no choice!

This is simply so important that you have to overcome your fear of confrontation and have that talk. The good news is we've got a plan that's going to make this negotiating business a cinch—and the icing is that, as Stephanie found, you usually get what you want, even with the toughest-sell bosses.

Underpinning you entire negotiating strategy is a simple tactic—you have to sell this as a win/win. Your bosses will usually only sign on if they believe it makes good business sense for them as much as it makes good lifestyle sense for you. Here's how.

Rule One: Negotiate from a Position of Fact-Based Strength

You want to change your work schedule because the current hamster wheel is making your life intolerable. You may even be tempted to quit altogether but want to give your employers a shot at making it work. If so, you haven't really got a huge amount to lose. And even if you aren't ready to throw in the towel, or can't afford to, remember, you are of great value to them.

Have a quick skim over chapter 1 again. Remind yourself of all that female power. Remember how valuable we are in the workplace right now. How expensive we are to replace and how desperately our employers want just our kind of female management talents. In fact you have a lot less at stake in asking for a changed schedule than your employers do.

Feeling braver?

There's more to boost your confidence. Your boss's number

one concern will be that your productivity falls because you're not sitting at your desk. He or she will panic that you are lazing around on the company's paycheck with your head in the clouds and not in your work. It's an understandable concern. After decades of having employees within view and easily monitored, where every minute is accounted for, you are asking them to cede control of your day and simply trust you. No wonder they're apprehensive. But they don't need to be.

Remember—flexible workers are happy workers are more productive workers. We gave you this data in chapter 2, but here's one more stat: since Best Buy began its company-wide alternative work program—ROWE (Results-Only Work Environment)—productivity is up by an average of 41 percent, and in some departments, by 65 percent.

Best Buy bosses who were skeptical have become converts purely because the business results are so compelling. John "J.T." Thompson, an old-school, watch-the-clock kind of guy and senior vice president of BestBuy.com was a huge skeptic. J.T. came of age believing anyone who didn't live in her office wasn't a team player. He loved nothing more than a Sunday afternoon at his desk. At first he pushed back against the architects of ROWE, Cali Ressler and her co-conspirator Jody Thompson (no relation to J.T.). He dismissed their revolutionary flexibility plan as nothing more than a New Age slackers club.

"I was not supportive," says J. T. Thompson. In fact he wasn't just "not supportive," he was downright terrified about losing control. J.T. was convinced employees would use the program to draw a salary without doing the work. How are you going to measure productivity? he wanted to know.

But one of J.T.'s managers reassured him with a set of concrete performance metrics. They would be able to measure how many orders per hour the team was processing, no matter where they were. The manager promised J.T. he'd haul everyone back into the office if orders dipped for a second. Reluctantly, J.T. agreed to give it a shot.

Within a month the team's productivity was up, and engagement scores (those job satisfaction and retention measures) were the highest in the history of the whole division. J.T. had always worried about engagement scores, and when he saw these numbers he was thrilled. He moved fast to implement the system in the entire online sales department. Voluntary turnover fell from over 16 percent to zero. "For years I had been focused on the wrong currency," Thompson confesses. "I was always looking to see if people were here. I should have been looking at what they were getting done."

J.T.'s experience is shared by everyone we have talked with who has embraced alternative work schedules.

At Capitol One, Senior Vice President Judy Pahren says it just makes sense. Simply being in the office doesn't mean you're being productive—far from it. "If an employee is in the office but is actually worried about their child getting off the bus OK and doing their homework properly," says Pahren, "they're not actually focusing on work because they're distracted by their kid. It is much better for that person to leave early and catch up on e-mails and project work from home in the evening. That person will actually be more productive in that hour and a half than they would be if they had spent it here worrying about things going at home."

And this dynamic is certainly not confined to parents. Pahren cites the example of an associate who uses her alternative work schedule to spend afternoons involved in community service. Being able to fulfill her charitable commitments makes the associate a happier, more satisfied person—which in turn makes her a more productive person in all areas of her life, including her work.

All of this, from women's power in the marketplace to the

increased productivity that flexible schedules can generate, will help you make an impressive case. And remember, you've probably spent huge chunks of your career persuading people to do what you want. You persuade the boss to pursue a client, a client to sign on their account, a colleague to join a project. You, in fact, are the expert at turning data and facts into a fluid, persuasive argument.

The fact is, you already have the power of professional persuasion in your back pocket. You just need to use it for yourself.

Rule Two: Perform Well and Know It

Managers told us repeatedly that they would bend over backward to retain women who add value. It seems obvious to us. You are in a much stronger position to demand the work life you want if your company wants to keep you. Let's not kid ourselves. If your bosses think you're of marginal benefit, they're going to be happier to let you go than to disrupt their carefully organized office routine to satisfy you.

Chances are, however, that you do add value, and we suspect your biggest problem, as a woman, is *not* that you don't perform but that you don't appreciate just how needed you are. That's the case for the vast majority of women we've spoken to.

However, just to be sure, take stock of your performance—in any job there are ways to measure performance. How are your annual appraisals? Do you meet your sales targets? Have your bosses complimented your work? Are you someone they turn to with confidence? Do you shape the discussion at your company strategy meetings? Do they happily put you in front of clients? Have you been promoted recently? Do you get face-time with higher-ups? How easy would it be to replace you? You may need to spend a number of months making yourself invaluable.

If you're feeling at all nervous, chuck a little confidence and pride into the negotiating mix. We love Linda Brooks' story about how she negotiated her two-thirds law partner deal—almost unheard of in her circles.

Linda simply gave them no wiggle room, and it worked. "I said, 'I have to go flextime, I want flextime.' Actually, I don't even think they would have negotiated if I had said it in less stark terms," she admits. "But I just said, 'This is what I want to do,' and they said, 'Specifically, what percentage of time off do you want,' because with our firm it's all a time-percentage thing, and I said, 'Two-thirds time.' Which means I leave a third of the profits behind. And they said, 'For how long?' and I said, 'Indefinitely.' They were convinced then, I'm sure, that it was just a passing phase." She laughs. "But now I can't ever see myself going back, I'm happier than I've ever been."

For women in their thirties and forties, this is *the* time to really push for your New All because your stock has never been higher. You have years of super valuable experience in your field and quite possibly years in your company too. You can't be replaced by an inexperienced twenty-five-year-old, and your company needs your longevity. So these are the years to max out on your value and demand all the time you need. Linda Brooks was nearing forty and already a partner when she got her new life—it was the ideal time to up the ante: "I got what I wanted because I already had power. So what were they going to do?"

Rule Three: **Never Negotiate in Anger**

That *never* is serious advice. We mean never. You cannot negotiate something as important as your whole work life in the heat of anger. But let's face it, this is an issue that gets our hormones going and our emotions raised.

Imagine you've had a really bad day, one of those days when

you felt close to quitting. Your boss has kept you in the office way later than you'd like. You missed a parent-teacher conference. You missed homework. You missed your Pilates class. You missed dinner with your spouse. You missed calling your mom, and it's her birthday. You got home too late for bedtime, and little Chloe cried, the sitter tells you disapprovingly. And to top it all off, your boss chewed you out for not meeting the deadline (which she'd only given you that morning) and turning in substandard work (even though this was a two-day project jammed into one day). Yes, one of those days. In the privacy of your car on the drive home you finally let the tears flow. You've had enough, you can't bear spending this much time in the office for so little return. You're going to go in next morning, tell her you are way overstretched, and demand a different schedule.

Don't. At least don't do it the next morning.

There is no point negotiating in anger. Negotiations are stressful enough, so it is worth waiting until the heat has subsided. An employee who comes in angry and upset seems out of control and unprofessional. Your boss will probably end up thinking she was quite right to chew you out.

No, you need to wait a few days, even a few weeks if necessary, and go into those critical negotiations calm and cool. You may not really feel that way, but you've got a better chance of faking it if there's some distance between you and that day from hell.

Rule Four: Know What You're Asking For

Decide beforehand exactly what you want your work life to look like and write it down. We've given you quite a few examples in this book of different women working different ways. There are literally thousands of schedule permutations. Before you put draw up your ideal, here are a few lifestyle issues to think of.

Do you need time with your children after school?

Do you want a regular morning every week to take a parent to the doctor?

Do you have family abroad and need more vacation time to visit them?

Do you simply hate putting on panty hose and a suit and long instead for the relaxed atmosphere of working from your kitchen table?

Do you have a bad commute? Could you save valuable hours by avoiding the morning rush hour and arriving late?

Go back to chapter 3 and take that Womenomics gut check test again—be clear about what you really want. Think through all the permutations and work out what suits your needs, while of course keeping your business' requirements firmly in mind.

Now look at the schedule options.

The first question is: Do you want to work full time or part time? Here you need to work out whether yours is a job that could realistically shift from five days to four days, with that extra day really being "off." If you can guarantee that your Fridays or Mondays, whichever day it is, will be undisturbed by work, and you can afford the pay cut, this can be a great option— and a particularly appealing one for your boss during a recession. But before you opt for the pay cut, calculate the risk that you may end up working that extra day anyway, even if you aren't paid for it.

Beyond part time there are plenty of creative ways to squeeze a full-time job into fewer hours in the office. Would a full work-week compressed into fewer days (four times ten hours is a popular option) suit you? Would working from home for one, two, or three days a week cut down on commute time and leave you free for school pickup? Do you want to start supper early and leave the office every day at 3 P.M.—or never get in before midday but work until late at night?

Be flexible; you may initially think one arrangement is ideal but in time find something else works better. When Melissa James at Morgan Stanley went to her boss six years ago, she thought she wanted to work part-time. She suggested she'd like to work three days a week, and he was surprisingly open to that. They took some time and created an internal job for her that entailed less travel and client time. But over time, her responsibilities grew, she was enjoying her new role, and her viewpoint changed. "I was gaining an appreciation for the fact that what I needed in terms of workplace flexibility was not necessarily a quote-unquote 'part time' or 'reduced' work schedule, I needed more flexibility and control, which is what I think a lot of women in the workplace actually need these days. They don't necessarily need to work part time, but they do need an ability to control their schedule to some degree."

Now she's back to a high-profile full-time gig, but it provides flexibility in terms of school events and other family obligations.

"You know it's not always the best thing to be working three or four days," Melissa maintains. "Sometimes it's actually better to be working five days a week but to be able to be home or able to do something outside of work when you need to."

And don't be put off by a fusty corporate culture. You can make changes to your schedule even in the most rigid of companies. For energy executive Sarah Slusser, who has hired dozens of associates in her two-decade career and has seen changes in organizations not known for their modern attitudes, clarity, confidence, and commitment are the three essential Cs.

"If it's not an enlightened organization, if it's a place that has all these antiquated rules, and if you really want the flexibility that I think is necessary to raise a family properly, then I think you really need to do that personal assessment," she says. "Everyone has a different need. I don't think anyone's is the same.

And then ask for it and live up to your commitments. You have to say, look I'm going to commit to these hours or get this kind of work done, but I need this kind of flexibility in exchange. If you live up to your commitments and you don't over promise, then I think you gain a lot of credibility by addressing it up front instead of sneaking out every Friday because you need to pick up the kids."

You do the analysis. Be both realistic and creative. See what would put the sanity back in your frazzled life. Now write it down.

Rule Five: Be Prepared to Reassure Your Boss, on Every Level

Bosses are worriers. They can't help it. Bear with them. When it comes to granting flexibility we've found most of their concerns boil down to that one simple question: How will I know you won't just play with the kids and lounge around at home on the company's payroll eating Doritos all day? We know, it's very tempting to say—"for God's sake, just trust me, I'm a grown-up who takes her commitments seriously." But to get your New All, you'll have to give a more concrete reassurance than that. Here's our list of reassurances to wield. Once you fire off a few of these, his misguided notions will vanish.

1. "I Will Be More Productive and Therefore This Change Will Help Both Me and the Company"

Tell your boss why you want this change. Say how much you love your work but that you need more control over your time. Then provide evidence for how the new situation will not detract from your performance; indeed you believe the company will benefit because you will be less stressed and more committed to your work.

We've shown you the national data on how flexibility increases productivity. Now make that specific to your situation. You can use benchmarks as a concrete way to frame this fact. To show that you've thought this through, create a fairly detailed outline that is designed to show your boss that this is a positive move. You can use productivity measures, or you can simply use an ongoing project as your performance goal, outlining that after one month on your new schedule you'll have completed specific parts of the project. Benchmarks like these will show in hard terms that the flexibility plan is a solid one. (We have some examples of just how to measure results later in this chapter.)

It can also be extremely helpful to find a way to frame your negotiations so that your flexible schedule helps solve a company problem:

- In this uncertain economy, your company is going through budget issues, and you want to go part time. Your new schedule is a great way to help cut costs.

- Your company needs to extend its hours to deal with Europe and Asia, and you want to leave at 3 P.M. to pick the kids up from school. Offer to come in at 6 A.M. and solve their early-morning time needs.

- Your company is growing fast and needs extra office space. Working from home will free up a desk.

- New managers need training and development. If you reduce your workload you can pass on a valuable opportunity to someone else.

If you can sell this as a win-win you are almost guaranteed a positive reception. Kathleen Christensen has a useful mental tip here. When you're negotiating your new deal, think of it in your *own mind* as a business strategy, not a favor.

"I would say that anyone negotiating it has to change their mind-set away from flexibility being an accommodation, a benefit, a perk, to seeing it as a strategic business tool," Christensen explains. "And therefore when they propose it, they have to show how it's going to enhance business as well as their own work lives, and maybe then their retention. I think one of the problems is that too many people for too long have seen these as entitlements that will make their personal lives better, but that there's no recognition of what the consequences will be for their team and for the organization in general, for meeting deadlines, and being productive."

2. "I've Got an Iron-Clad, Detailed Plan"

It's also important to have a concrete plan for how your new schedule will work in practice. For example, how will you continue communicating with other team members and, if necessary, with clients? If you have a job where rapid client response is important, this is likely to be a key concern for your boss. No one wants to think a hotshot, well-paying client is going to be kept waiting while you take five-hour hikes in the Adirondacks.

If you want to work from home and telecommute, describe your home-office setup and reassure your boss up front that children will be taken care of full time. Offer to pay for any technology upgrades. Remember, you're trying to sell this as a good deal for them too, so spin it as positively as you can.

When litigation lawyer Jennifer Keisling interviewed with her boss, Dorothy O'Brien, the vice president and deputy general counsel of legal and environmental affairs at E.ON U.S., she had specific lifestyle demands. She was pregnant, and knew already she'd want to work part time. Having had a very successful run at the U.S. Department of Justice, she was being courted by several top law firms. She made a compelling case for being flexible about her less-than-full-time status. O'Brien wanted this important fish—still, she worried about reeling her in.

"Let me tell you the primary concern. When you're in a professional position where you are providing a service to others in the business, we pride ourselves on immediate availability and responsiveness. But how do you fit a part-time employee into that paradigm? I don't want to be in a position where we've agreed to a one-to-five schedule and a crisis comes up when she's not there. When you're a professional, you need to be available. But how do you reconcile that availability with the core agreement that we've reached?"

O'Brien hired her, and has been thrilled with the payoff. "I think it was a leap of faith," she says. "And it proved to be worth the risk, on both sides." Indeed, over time, Jennifer, a committed Christian, decided she wanted to homeschool her now three children. More than a grand title, or even a grander salary, she was eager to have mornings off to teach her children. It's certainly an unusual arrangement for a top lawyer, but Jennifer convinced Dot that she had every detail worked out. She had help from her in-laws at home in case she had to come in, she had her home wired for working from there at odd hours, and she said she was willing to take calls in the mornings if necessary. And she'd already shown, over the years, how artful she could be at making flexibility work.

O'Brien, already thrilled with Jennifer's contributions, said yes. "If Jennifer's needed here, she works it out. And then we figure out how to equalize things at the back end," she explains. "If you have people who operate in good faith, who are really motivated to do a good job, they do it."

3. "I'm Offering Open, Honest Communication— Even about Money"

Don't pretend to be able to do things from home that you can't. We know an art historian who deals with precious manuscripts. If those medieval books leave the climate-controlled basement of her museum, they'll probably disintegrate. So, more than she'd really like, she simply has to be in the museum. What's the ancient tome in your job?

If there are elements of your job where face-time with colleagues (or manuscripts) is unavoidable, reassure your boss that you still intend to be there for those meetings. Let him or her know that you understand there will be times when telecommuting just won't work. Honesty makes your plan seem more realistic. And quell his jittery nerves by making it clear that you will give everyone plenty of notice of your availability. (Remember, you're dealing with an anxious child here. Treat with caution!)

You may want to try to go flexible before you go part time. Losing money should always be the last option. But if that is what makes sense, and that is what you want, then YOU need to make it clear in these negotiations exactly what you expect financially. Many bosses worry you'll be looking for "special treatment." You need to be open about the fact that you are not expecting to produce less without taking less money. You are looking for a fair deal, and all details can be discussed openly.

4. "I Will Be Flexible, Too"

Emphasize that you will be flexible with your flexibility.

For Christine Heenan, half of whose ten-person communications team works on flexible schedules, reciprocity is essential. She doesn't really care when or where her employees work, so long as they get the job done. She has bent over backward to accommodate her associates' schedules, but she also expects them to adapt their schedules if there's a company emergency.

"I think knowing that there is flexibility within their flexibility is very important. So for example, I have this new employee, Kim, who works Monday, Wednesday and Friday. I got a call yesterday on my way to Washington D.C. saying the mayor's office had set up a project meeting for us for this morning at 9 A.M., not knowing that I was out of town. And so I called Kim and said, 'Kim, I can't do this meeting, can you?' And she said, 'Yep, I just need some background.' I didn't start the conversation by saying, 'I know you don't work on Tuesdays,' she didn't start her response with, 'Well Tuesday is not normally a day I work.' But there is going to be a Friday that Kim has to be somewhere else and we'll work it out. I think that if you're rigid about the flexibility that you've demanded, that's problematic. Flexibility has to go both ways," says Heenan.

Offer contingency plans for possible conflicts. If there's a crunch at work and you need to work on Friday, even though you usually have it off, make it clear that you can do so. Suggest that you'd be happy to take that day off the following week when things have calmed down in the office.

Angelique Krembs, a marketing director at PepsiCo who's been with the company for fifteen years, just returned to work full time after two years of working from home on a project basis. The situation worked extremely well, largely because both she and the company tried hard to meet each other's requirements.

"It has to be a two-way street," she says. "Pepsi showed me enormous flexibility, and so I showed it to them too."

She'd been dreading the company's response when she told them she was just not ready to come back after an extended maternity leave. "I thought I would have to resign," she remembers. The response floored her. "Tell us what would make it work for you," her HR person responded. "I was surprised," she admits. And gratified. And the company was open again when she told them she was pregnant again and asked to extend her work-from-home situation. And in return, she says, when they asked her to handle a project that kept her much busier for a number of months than she would have liked, she was happy to do it.

And now PepsiCo has a valuable employee back at headquarters.

5. "We'll Directly Measure My Results, First during a Trial Period"

We've told you your boss will want to know you will be as productive, if not more so. Therefore, when you work your own schedule it is even more important to be able to assess results. So reassure your boss by giving her concrete suggestions for measuring your performance, even when you are not in her line of sight.

Here are some ways to think about what exactly you might propose to measure, and how:

At Best Buy, Jody Thompson found sorting this out to be easier than she had thought. "Everything can be measured. What we found is that things that are subjective can be measured as well," she says. "So if I'm doing something that's knowledge work-based, it could be measured on customer service or internal customer satisfaction." And forcing your company to define your role can have huge strategic benefits by really creating a focus on who does what and why. She adds, "In a more flexible environment, when you're not counting hours for an employee, you really have to think to yourself, 'Why does this person exist, what are they supposed to be doing for this company, and how can I measure that, because I'm not using putting in time as a measurement anymore.' We've seen that every single person can find a way to measure their output," Jody adds.

Here's one very concrete example of those benchmarks we mentioned earlier. This is how Chandra Dhandapani sets goals for her employees at Capital One, and it shows how specific they can be.

"One of my associates manages a back office function of about eighty associates and a couple of key vendors. I have set specific objectives for her including:

a) manage the budgets and make sure all costs and expenses stay within our budget commitments

b) achieve 100 percent adherence to Service Level Agreements on customer need resolution—i.e., resolve any customer escalations within a set time frame

c) establish a Quality Assurance function to drive appropriate balance across Customer Experience, Efficiency, and Effectiveness (CEEE).

In addition, I also measure associate engagement scores and associate morale scores for her team on a quarterly basis."

Chandra doesn't care where this associate works from or even how many hours she works, so long as she achieves those results.

"Since I measure her success based on clear targets and milestones, I don't have to worry about the time she clocks or where she works from," she says. "This arrangement works well for both of us, and she is one of our consistent high performers. I would say that in my experience, associates tend to go above and beyond when they feel that the company cares about them as individuals and they don't see their work-life arrangement as a win-lose."

In a less quantifiable environment, of course, it's trickier but still possible. Christy Runningen of Best Buy, who is a performance coach at the company, says that the goals she works out with her boss tend to be a mix of how many people she might be able to help ideally in a given week, and also some of the softer scale measurements like the quality of the advice and the help she's dispensing. That data is collected in an anecdotal fashion from employees and colleagues.

"We try to find that middle ground to measure," she explains. "Some number that is tangible and easy to look at, because those soft stories are great, but we are a numbers-based company."

If you can offer metrics like those, and then propose a trial period, say three months, with a formal review at the end, who could say no? And the trial period is the key closer. Most people will be happy to sign up for a new scheme for that short period, especially if they know there's a chance to change aspects of the schedule later. And the fact is, if you do it well, it's awfully hard for them to reverse what you already have in place.

Rule Six: Remember—You're Dealing with a Jittery Child. There Will Be Worries You Haven't Even Thought Of

Let's give your higher-ups more time in the Womenomics sun and really examine some of the less obvious worries employers have about flexibility. We think you can address most of them fairly easily, but we wouldn't be arming you with valuable information if we didn't slip into the top dog's shoes for a while and warn you about corporate fears you may not even have thought of.

This Will Open Pandora's Box

This may be the biggest unspoken fear for all bosses who might want to consider a broader policy—the domino effect. "If I give it to Jane then Sharon will want it too," they tell us, "and then where do I stop? Soon the whole office is working at the time and place of their choosing." Oh my God, man the barricades, it is the spread of the Alternative Work Schedule revolution! Heaven save us from the Pink Terror!

He may not even let you know this is why he's wavering, but if it seems appropriate, you can subtly drop this point: one huge U.S. company that has done research on this very issue found there is no risk of a major moral hazard. Accountants Deloitte and Touche have a bold company-wide flexible work program, but they have found that at any one moment only 10 percent of the staff actually opts in. The other 90 percent are happy with a traditional work structure. The dominos are mostly still standing tall.

Can I Reward Polly but Not Pam?

"What happens if I think Emily is great and I want to keep her so I give her the precious telecommute she asks for, but Anna isn't so great, so I don't want to accommodate her schedule?" is a similar boss concern.

Valerie Jarrett says that's exactly what she found when she was running Habitat. "My first thought is being fair," she says. "If you're creating an exception for somebody, then first you have to figure out what you're going to do if everybody wants that same exception, and would it work system-wide or can you justify the distinction."

Michael Nannes is the managing partner of the powerhouse law firm Dickstein Shapiro in Washington, D.C. He's also a demigod for in-the-know female lawyers, because he's created a firm that embraces flexibility and the goal of giving lawyers lives. He realized when he had children of his own that having time to be there for them was important, so he's more than happy to accommodate other people's different schedules. He has one lawyer who takes all summer off to coach her child's swim team. "If you get your work done, that's what counts."

But even he says there are times when the policy can be awkward. "You get problem cases where somebody who's not doing that well goes and opts for a part-time situation. As an employer, you do bang your head on that one," says Michael Nannes.

Still, in Nannes's experience, the alternative schedule discussion can have the benefit of prompting a useful conversation about the employee's overall performance. "On a couple of occasions that's precipitated an honest discussion about the person's career track," says Nannes.

Our take? You might not be able to say this out loud, but the Anna-isn't-so-great issue is a red herring. It needs to be dealt with as a performance issue not as a flexibility issue. Make your pitch based on your top performance, and you'll be the one to get the good deal.

Face-Time Matters

Workplace expert Tory Johnson, CEO of Women for Hire, says some in-person time is important to many employers. "I do think that there are benefits for all of our careers and for our personal growth and development to have access to meetings," she explains. "You get a chance to demonstrate your skills and your knowledge to an audience that perhaps you don't deal with on a regular basis. It's exposure to new people and new ideas."

Valerie Jarrett, who ran the Habitat Company before going to the White House, says she prefers to actually see people. "I'm totally addicted to e-mail, but I don't like to have a lot of serious conversations by e-mail. I like people to get up, walk out of their office, go down the hall, sit down, and talk to one another. So much of it depends on trust and relationships and doing things together, and I think that we get better product when we have that."

Michael Nannes has critical advice to anyone who thinks they can just work from home *all* the time—your boss won't like it, and with good reason.

"I mean look, you want to be available. You want to be seen. Face-time isn't irrelevant. You want to be down the hall when there's a new matter coming in or there's a new development and people sit around in the office or in a conference room and start to think about it and start knocking ideas around—being here is helpful."

So as you think about your ideal schedule, and wonder why *everything* can't be done remotely, remember that bosses have legitimate reasons for wanting you around sometimes. Don't underestimate a boss's love of a good meeting!

It's More Work for Me

Your boss may well be concerned that managing employees who come in nine-to-five is so much more simple than managing individual work arrangements and that your flexible plan may well mean more work for him. That's why some of the biggest flextime skeptics are the middle managers, who will have to handle a lot of it, and who would often prefer the easy way out. Bruce Tulgan says that there's no question managers might need some reeducation. "Managers still like to pay a lot of attention to where people are because that is easiest to measure," explains Tulgan. "It's visible. Otherwise, you have to be really good at managing results, and that is harder. But the upside is it's better for business."

Remember to outline how easy you will make this for him, and that a shift toward focusing on results may ultimately make him look brilliant.

The Clients Won't Stand for It

This is especially true at law firms and investment banks and high-profile corporations, and it's one reason why some blue chip firms have been so slow to offer anything resembling a healthy work-life balance. "It's a problem because many of the firms just don't want to let the client know their attorney is working less than full time," says Deborah Epstein Henry, president of Flex-Time Lawyers.

But major law firms are discovering that clients can be trained. More and more of them offer part-time partnerships, and the fact is, lawyers usually have to juggle a number of cases at once—so in reality, clients often have to wait for a response anyway. If you are valuable to your clients you have enough leverage to pull it off.

Rule Seven: Use Economics to Your Advantage

In a Womenomics world an economic downturn can be upturned to your advantage. We've said this before, but it bears repeating. Don't let glum economic headlines convince you that this is the wrong time to ask for anything. Bosses everywhere will be looking for ways to cut costs, so if you are proposing a work relationship that will save him a bit of salary costs, you'll probably get an immediate yes. Or if you are simply looking to work more flexibly, you may also get a thumbs-up—especially as supervisors are looking for ways to reward workers that don't involve cash.

So think carefully about what you want and, again, what your company needs right now. Use it all in your negotiation.

"Bob—I understand that the usual bonuses will be hard to come by this year—and I'd like to offer you an alternative. I'd certainly see it as a sign of your confidence in me and your happiness with my performance if we could create a situation where I work from home two days a week."

Or—"Virginia. I know what the company is going through right now. And I know real estate is at a premium and that you're looking for office space. What if we turn this into a win-win for everyone—and I work from home most days, and our new vice president can have my office."

Or—"Charles. I know you're struggling with these potential layoffs. Remember how I proposed a four-day workweek last year? What if we give that a go now? It could take some of the pressure off the company."

CLAIRE   For years I'd somehow managed to craft an "unofficial" flexible relationship with my company. After my first child, I proposed a four-day workweek, but the higher-ups didn't think it made sense because of my profile at the company. ABC did let me work from home a good bit though, and I was told that face-time in the office didn't have to be a priority, which helped enormously as I tried to balance it all. Still, I always hoped to make the arrangement more formal—to literally trade money for time—so that I could shake some of the guilt I often felt when I'd turn down an assignment or travel, but ABC just didn't want to go that route. Until last year. As I was writing this book—the finances at our company grew increasingly tight. It turned out to be the perfect opening to make a new deal that, yes, cut my salary (ouch), but also my hours and the demands on my time. It's working well for all of us, and I'm sure the company might not have considered it if they weren't looking at a new financial reality.

Cynthia Trudell, the senior vice president and head of personnel at PepsiCo, says a recession is the ideal time for companies to focus on efficiency and potential savings.

"Your own employees might decide they want to take some time off and work differently, and they're likely far more valuable than a consultant, so that can be extremely effective."

Rule Eight: Now That You've Got Your Deal, Don't Take It for Granted, or, "It's the Communication, Stupid"

Once you've secured your great work life don't slip into balanced bliss and assume you can park your schedule in the DONE file and expect everyone to be permanently delighted. Your precious New All is a high-maintenance tropical flower—heavenly but demanding.

- Obviously you do need to keep performing. You can't go into this deal a fast-tracker and a year later find yourself stalling in the slow lane and expect no one to notice. Whether it's at the coffee shop, in your kitchen, or at the beach house, you do actually need to keep justifying that salary. Sorry!

- Make a point of regularly checking in with your higher-ups to ensure they're still on board. There is nothing worse than going into the office one day and finding your boss has revoked your at home/day off/short week privileges because of a simmering discontent that you had no idea about.

- Take the initiative about keeping in touch. Remind colleagues that even though you're not physically present, you fully expect them to call you whenever necessary. Why not go one step further and make a point of calling them just to break the ice.

Chandra Dhandapani's system at Capital One is so brilliant for women because it is completely the norm. Not only is there a formula for measuring results, as we described above, but there is also an equally rigorous system for maintaining employee/employer communication to keep those targets on track. The company has instituted regular communication between associates and their bosses known as ten-ten meetings in which each side gets ten minutes to express any concerns or queries.

"Ten tens are always one-on-one meetings between a manager and their direct reports and are typically held once a week or once every two weeks. I use mine to:

- Check in with my direct reports on high-level progress against their goals—this is not a detailed work review meeting. (I set up separate weekly check-ins to review key metrics and progress on key initiatives.)

- Check in on how they are doing on an individual level—their mood, stress level, workload, and any help they need from me in removing roadblocks.

- Exchange feedback—this is a two-way conversation where I give them feedback on how they are doing overall from my vantage point, and they give me feedback on our interaction, the direction of the department, or anything else that's on their mind."

Remember, you're doing something different, and sometimes people find that awkward, almost embarrassing, so the onus is on you to keep those lines open and easy. Melissa James at Morgan Stanley says bosses find this communicating issue one of the trickiest issues to deal with when someone is working from home.

"People don't know how to have an honest dialogue about this stuff," Melissa said. She also told us that managers are often thinking, "'What should I say? How should I say it?' If this person has asked for workplace flexibility, I don't want to put too many demands on them, so if I ask them to do something is it going to be OK? Like, for example, I have heard of situations where women are working from home on a particular day, but nobody feels comfortable calling them, and that only exacerbates the situation. It makes people feel uncomfortable. I think some managers are nervous about trying these work arrangements because they're afraid of what the expectations are going to be."

Jennifer Keisling, the part-time attorney who works for Dot O'Brien in Louisville, Kentucky, agrees that a critical element is communication. Sometimes that involves communication about what you can't do.

"You have to have the flexibility to say no to specific things without there being pressure on you at all. I need to be able to say I'm going to offload this to outside counsel, with no second-guessing." She tries to think of the mutual flexibility this way:

"I am committed to doing this job and fulfilling the mutual goals that we have, and doing my best at it, while also being flexible on the other end, on the home side too," explains Jennifer. "I'm willing to do all of that, but when I say I can't do something, I need to be able to say no."

The trick, obviously, is to let bosses know you're available and committed—without being available and committed the whole time! If you've got a terrific boss, it will work fine. Otherwise, you'll soon know whether they're abusing the situation, and then you need to address that. And all of it will be easier if you've been in regular communication about how it's working.

Here Are a Few Telltale Signs That Your Deal Isn't Making Your Boss Happy

Problem: That stream of high-profile projects you're used to working on starts drying up.

Solution: Bring it up and ask why. Is your boss unhappy with your performance, or is it just out of sight, out of mind? Find a way to get back on the radar and keep that performance level high, high, high.

Problem: Key decisions are made without you.

Solution: Find out if it's just because you were off that day or whether there's a bigger problem. Don't get paranoid, but do keep communicating with your colleagues and your boss. Maybe you need to see whether there are key decisions happening regularly on your day off and adjust your schedule or call in to that essential meeting.

Problem: Someone less qualified is promoted over you.

Solution: Ask why. Is your performance slipping, or is your special deal undermining your value? Communication is a two-way street, but the onus is on you to keep the traffic flowing. You know you will have to recalibrate short-term expectations if you are working less time, but if you feel this was undeserved, you need to schedule face-time with your employers and check whether or not the deal is still working for them.

It keeps coming back to talking about everything—on all levels. Melissa has an employee who works from home on Fridays, but occasionally she'll need her to come in anyway on that day. "I'm not afraid to tell her, 'Look, you've got to tell me if this isn't working for you. If somehow this isn't working I need to hear it from you, because I don't want to be playing a guessing game or trying to read your mind. And vice versa, if it's not working for me, I have to tell you as well.'"

Melissa James and Chandra Dhandapani couldn't work in more different industries or in more different companies. One is an investment banker, the other an auto loan officer. One is in New York, the other is in Plano, Texas. One has had to negotiate and create her own flexibility in a world where it is totally the exception. The other was offered nirvana from scratch—she's lucky enough to work for a company where eight-to-six in an office sounds, well, neanderthal. But these two determined, successful women share one unwavering belief when it comes to maintaining their own treasured work lives and making flexibility work for those below them: just as with marriage, kids, friends, and life—*it is all about communication.*

Rule Nine: Know When to Quit

Look, we'll be candid—it can happen that rules one through eight just don't work. And that's when you need rule nine. Sometimes, however skillfully you make your case, your boss just won't be able to overcome the worry list. When you really have tried everything and still can't get the work life you want from a boss who just won't budge, you know it's time to quit.

Christy Runningen of Best Buy had come to that realization before she landed in a ROWE. When she was suffering from those back-to-work Sunday evening blues you read about earlier, she was trying everything she could think of to carve out time in her life to be with her kids. The stress levels were getting unbearable. You'll remember, she had permission to work "summer hours," a system that theoretically allowed her to squeeze her full-time workweek into four and a half days. She would go in very early Monday morning, work hard until Friday noon, and then take that afternoon off with the children.

"I was calculating all of my time and hours and saying, 'Yeah, I have over forty-five hours in by lunchtime on Friday,'" she recalls. "I was just so excited to be able to take my daughter to the pool, just spend the afternoon with her."

But her boss kept giving her grief. "He kept saying, 'I'm here late, so you should be here late too.'" Christy was starting to panic. "I thought this is not a balance for me and this is not the way I want to live my life. Nitpicking the number of hours that they are seeing me here; or proving that I'm only leaving my desk for a half hour for lunch, just so I can scrape together some time so that I can be with my daughter."

She started making plans to leave the company and was considering a job as a day care provider, desperate to escape the prison-like stress. In the end she was rescued. The manager left first. Poetic justice. She moved to another team, joined one of Best Buy's ROWEs, and hasn't looked back. "It's like the heavens opened up," she says, laughing. But if chance hadn't intervened, Christy knows she would have been out the door.

For Jennifer Winell, quitting meant leaving not just her job but also giving up on years of training as an orthopedic surgeon. It was her passion. It was also a field where women are extremely rare—less than five percent of all orthopedic surgeons are women. After qualifying, Jennifer ended up at a tough New York hospital where she was on call constantly—even more than the other surgeons, because she was the only pediatric specialist there. "It was just unbelievably stressful, and I was like Pavlov's dog. When my beeper went off my heart would start racing, and I just felt, 'Oh my God, I can't do this,'" she remembers.

Over the course of her two years at the hospital she tried to tweak things around the edges to win a little more control, but there was a massive expectations gap. Jennifer knew that one day she'd like to get married and have kids, but it was also very clear to her that in that profession, which she calls the ultimate old boys club, she'd never be able to get the flexibility she needed to have a family. "It would never have even crossed my mind to ask for something like that," she remembers. "It would have been unheard of."

Jennifer ultimately decided not only to quit but also to take some time off so she could choose her next move with greater realism. She researched hospitals, practices, and the entire field of orthopedics. Eventually she decided she had to give up operating, after six years of training. She joined a team that gives her a four-day workweek, and she evaluates cases that might require surgery. Along the way she got married and had a baby. "There are definitely parts of my old career that I miss," she admits, talking about surgical practice, "but at the same time it's worth it to me to never be constantly on call again."

As with everything else, there are good ways to quit and bad ways to quit. We suggest you resist the Scarlett O'Hara impulse to flounce out and bang the door. Here are some tips for quitting with dignity, in a way that burns no bridges:

1. *Do* pick a day when you can control your emotions. Yes, we're trying to embrace our deepest feminine selves in this book, but a departure without tears is SO much classier, and SO much more commanding.

2. *Do* be clear about the reasons for your departure, and be overwhelmingly positive, yes, even about that job

you hate and are now leaving. "Bob, I'm so sorry to have to tell you this, but after a lot of thought, I've decided it's time for me to move on. We've had a terrific working relationship, and we've brought in extraordinary business together, more than any of us expected, but I'm afraid I really can't compromise on the schedule requirements I spelled out. I hope you understand, and with any luck we'll get another chance to do deals together in the future." Focus on accomplishments, without bragging (let that annoying boss take credit), and mention your demands briskly and crisply. No long dramatics about school plays and carpools and the chaos that your life has become. You may yet cross paths again.

3. *Don't* be anything less than sure of your message and your goal. You have to mean it. If you still somehow believe this is part of the negotiation, and you are expecting a last-minute apology and an incredible offer from that troll-like creature in front of you, it will show.

4. *Do* know, however, that your superior may well be shocked ("What—leave this heaven on earth?"), panicked ("What is management going to say about me losing Sally"), or genuinely remorseful ("I didn't think we were heading here. I wonder if we can work this out"). You may be asked what it will take to keep you; in that case, calmly say you'll think it over, don't commit to anything immediately. Even though you've been through Womenomics training, that desire to please, to smooth things over, will be extremely tempting. Resist, at least temporarily.

5. *Do* think and think hard about the counteroffer. If they make a play to keep you, are they really going to make good on the things you've asked for? Or will it just be talk? Do you believe, despite their initial reluctance, that they can really change their ways? Sometimes corporate resistance, or the underlying Scrooge-like spirit of the company, is just too strong. Your gut should help you a lot here. Suggest a trial period if you are worried.

Quitting can feel traumatic we know, but there is a huge upside. It gives you a chance to start fresh, to find a company or field that is compatible with the kind of work life you really need. You owe it to your newly reconstructed Womenomics self to move on and find what you want. We'll show you how.

news you can use

1. Outline exactly how your proposed freedom will work. To the letter.

2. Use the economy to your advantage.

3. Anticipate your supervisor's concerns and answer them head on.

4. Know your Womenomics power and productivity stats cold.

5. Know when to quit, and how.

a womenomics world

I f this is your moment to move on, congratulations. If you've quit, been poached, or even been laid off, the future looks rosier than the past. You may be feeling nervous and insecure, but your prospects, and the prospects for all women yearning for workplace sanity, are better than ever. Across the country, companies are instituting flexibility as a standard work practice, which often does away with the need for those agonizing individual negotiations. You've embarked on your search at just the right time—the work life you want is within reach.

Instead of trying to make an existing job bend to fit what you need, you may be able to find a new model built to suit. No retrofitting! And by the way, this is the same for any of you being wooed or simply looking around for something better from your current perch. In this chapter you'll learn not only how to spot potential employers that meet your needs, but we'll also show you our favorite Womenomics-friendly companies. Their example is changing our world of work.

A Fresh Start

If you're looking for a fresh start, the trick is to find out whether your potential mate is really everything he says he is. How do you know for sure this is a company that's going to suit your Womenomics requirements? When you're considering a new employer it's easy, of course, to ask about the job itself; it's a lot harder to ask about the firm's commitment to work-life issues. So how do you go about the hunt without scaring off the prey?

Here's some advice from an unexpected source.

Just as we were finishing this book, we checked in again with all of our women to see how they were doing, and we got some surprising news from Christine Heenan. Remember that when we first met Christine she was being wooed for a big job at Harvard and seemed pretty confident she would turn it down because she didn't want to give up her fantastically flexible work life at her own communications company in Rhode Island. Well, she changed her mind. The high-powered Harvard job was too exciting to resist. But here's the interesting thing: she only took that big job after pointedly raising her schedule requirements with the university.

At the end of her first interview with the search committee, Christine was asked if she had any questions. That's when she raised her work-life concerns and here's how she did it. "I said, 'I think it's probably fair to say that I work as much or as intensively as anyone at this table but I also think it's quite likely that I work differently. I'm at my kids' school at 3 o'clock most afternoons picking them up and I run a school newspaper project on Fridays and I value my flexibility. What is Harvard's commitment to work-life balance?'"

She knew the Harvard job would demand more hours in the office than she was used to, but she was also clear that if Harvard wasn't going to be able to try to accommodate her family commitments, she wouldn't take the post. Christine wouldn't have taken the job if Harvard had responded negatively to her family concerns. Christine also feels the fact that Harvard has a new President, Drew Gilpin Faust, who is herself a working mother, means her boss genuinely understands her priorities. She says that makes a big difference in making her flexibility a practice not just a policy. And she believes that, having raised the issue formally, if her new colleagues ever raise eyebrows when she leaves early, she can always remind them of their interview conversation.

This is the thing about Womenomics, and it's what makes the traditional ladder idea so ridiculous: there are times to scale back and times to ramp up, just as Christine did. But whatever stage you're in, it's worth making very sure that the new job fits your work-life goals. And remember: there is a big difference between policy and practice when it comes to flexibility.

Do your due diligence. This seems obvious, but it's worth a reminder. Check out the company you're thinking of joining on the Web, at your favorite social networking site, in the local paper. There are lots of great resources. We love the Sloan Foundation's Family and Work Institute. They've got piles of data and a family-friendly annual survey. Or try *Working Mother* magazine. They've been rating the top companies for us for twenty years.

Take cards or names of people you come across in interviews who might be good sources. Check out the company-related blogs. They can be a trove of candid information. Call anybody on-site who might be straightforward about responsibilities, and potential issues; that connection is invaluable. Ask other women at the company what the reality is. And by the way, the savvy employer expects to be checked out.

"I keep reminding managers here," says David Rodriguez, head of HR at Marriott, "we're being evaluated constantly.

Somewhere on the Internet there is a group of people sharing this information. You can't hide. You can't say 'I'm this type of company' and not expect you will be assessed."

Be rigorous on details. Any employer can point to a couple of women who job share or leave at 3 P.M. Or he could open up the company manual and point out their progressive-sounding policies. For example, 98 percent of law firms offer part-time or flextime scheduling. Actual usage rates? Five percent. "It just shows how incredibly stigmatized the schedules still are," says Flextime Lawyers' Deborah Epstein Henry.

Even if the company as a whole has a good approach to alternative work schedules, just make sure that attitude applies to the corner of the shop where you'll be working. "Sixty percent of the company you're looking at could be on some type of flexible work arrangement, but the department you may work in could have a manager who's totally opposed," warns Women for Hire's CEO, Tory Johnson.

Now, we hope you are feeling empowered by Womenomics, but you do still have to be smart about getting the most from your power. Please do not start any interview by leaning across the desk and demanding a job share. *It's important to know when to raise flexibility.* "It might be a way to be knocked out of the interview process to say, 'What I want to know first and foremost is what's your policy on flexibility,'" says Johnson.

Christine's advice about how and when to raise the issue in the course of your job search? "I think you do have to first establish yourself as having the work ethic and the DNA to do the job as it's required, before you have permission to say, 'What's the threshold for you for doing it a bit differently?'"

But she did raise it early because she was ambivalent about even taking the job. First Lady Michelle Obama likes to recount the story of having a babysitter crisis just as she was going for her interview as public liaison for the University of Chicago hospital system. At the last minute, she threw her daughter in the stroller and figured that, since this was partly why she was looking at this job, they needed to know she put her family first. She took her daughter to the interview—a ballsy move—and got the job. And before her husband ran for president she routinely skipped out for afternoon soccer games.

Melissa James says it's like any other sales presentation: you have to know your audience. "You need to know the most effective way to talk about it for the person who's listening. Try to figure that out. But my advice would probably be to put it on the table. It's important to calibrate expectations from the start."

So if you feel you've got plenty of muscle, raise it early. For most of us, it's probably good smarts to follow that old chestnut of a standard script: inquire about responsibilities, show off your knowledge of the company, subtly brag about your achievements and prowess, and express enormous enthusiasm for joining the team. Once they are charmed by you and your talent, that's the moment to test the waters with your potential bosses and HR. Clever phrases to break the ice from Tory Johnson: "Talk to me about the culture of your department. Talk to me about your policies around flexibility. What do schedules look like here? What are the work styles of the people I'd be working with?"

Whenever in the process you choose to make your point, it's far better to *get specific before you take the job* about both your intentions and expectations. Using everything you've uncovered in *Womenomics*, make sure *you* know exactly how you want to work, and then let them know what you'd like to do and how you plan to do it. Don't cross your fingers and think you'll "sort it out later." By then, patterns and habits will have been established. You don't get a chance to reset the stage of your work life very often. Grab it.

Womenomics-Friendly

It's getting harder for companies to disguise their true natures. You certainly won't be taken in by a superficial rouge job if you've followed the process we outlined above. You'll also find, as you really begin to look around, that a company's Womenomics-friendly attitude will shine through like a healthy glow. And the news is good. Flexibility is moving quickly from being a favor to being the industry standard. We've discovered in our research that there are myriad ways to create programs that make for a happier and freer workforce, but we've also noticed that those companies that do it best have one of these two traits: either a commitment to full-scale institutional flexibility, or thoroughly modern managers who understand that productivity and talent retention are essential. Here are some examples of what you should be looking for.

Nirvana Squared

There's just no better way to describe what some companies have pulled off on the freedom front. We've given you details about the great program at Capital One, and there are so many other visionary places. What sets them apart is the belief that flexibility should be an institutional practice—a standard across the company instead of a favor bestowed by paternalistic employers. Their routes to this enlightened state were different, but the results—the benefits—are stunningly clear.

Best Buy

Next time you need to buy a television or a computer and you hop down to the local Best Buy to make the purchase, remind yourself that this isn't an ordinary shopping expedition. You are heading into the belly of a workplace revolution.

Back in 2002 Cali Ressler and Jody Thompson were both human resources managers at Best Buy, back then a ferociously face-time, eight-to-five, Monday-through-Friday kind of place. But Thompson, a boomer, and Ressler, a Gen Xer, saw that the world outside the company fences was changing—becoming less static. And they saw also that the old-fashioned culture at Best Buy just wasn't working for them.

So they started dreaming of a workplace that would suit them and the new global environment. It would be a workplace where no one has to get permission to watch their kids' weekday soccer game. A workplace where people aren't promoted because they arrive early and stay late. A workplace where there is no when or where—just "how well." A workplace where performance is measured solely on the basis of results and not hours at the office.

Their dream is now a reality called ROWE—Results-Only Work Environment. In a ROWE *you* control where, when, and how long you work. So long as you meet your professional objectives, the way you spend your time is entirely your decision.

Ressler and Thompson knew they couldn't just go to their CEO and trot out their vision, so they met in private and rolled out ROWE by stealth. They organized tiny pilots and waited for an opportunity to go bigger. In 2003 they got that chance, and since then, in a remarkably short time, these two pioneering women have radically changed the Fortune 500 megacompany into a worker-friendly haven. They have given employees far more than flexibility—they have also given them freedom. Their clock-less, schedule-less, boundary-less system of working has radically changed lives. Now ROWEs have spread throughout the company.

"When Jody and I first came up with ROWE, we were focused on the corporate office environment, but today we're actually on the verge of beginning work with Best Buy retail to figure out how this will look in the retail stores. ROWE is not about not going to a workplace; it's about having control over your time. There are things in every environment that just don't make sense anymore, and they're making people stressed-out and feel like children, so we know that there's a huge opportunity outside the office environment for this," explains Cali Ressler.

Workers at Best Buy say they no longer know if they work fewer hours; they don't really care, and they've stopped counting. But they are much happier, and they are more productive. Right across the company, departments that adopted the ROWE revolution saw productivity rise by an average of 40 percent.

"At first, we took this on faith—that people wanted to be treated like adults, they wanted to be trusted to do their work in a way that makes sense for them, and that people would really step up to the plate if left free to do their work the way *they* thought best, not the way the company *let* them do it," says Jody Thompson.

"I don't come in to the office at eight and leave at five, there's no way. I have two mornings from about 8 A.M. until 1 P.M. where I'm not in the office at all because I'm studying for a master's," says Christy Runningen, of Best Buy. "I didn't ask for permission, and nobody cares. I still get my job done, and I'm happier and more productive than ever."

Naturally, Jody and Cali encountered hurdles. They've had to deal with old-fashioned managers who refused to cede control, with naysayers who said that it would never work and that productivity would plummet. The biggest concern for some managers was that employees would abuse the system— yet, overwhelmingly, that hasn't happened. Actually ROWE makes it easier, says Thompson, not harder, to see if associates are genuinely pulling their weight rather than just spending long hours in the office.

"The only way that you can scam a results-only work environment is to not get your job done," explains Thompson. "And, really, what happens on teams is that people who aren't pulling their weight weren't doing it before. In ROWE, it becomes really evident, and people are managed strictly on performance, so if somebody's not holding up their end, it becomes really clear. But they could just skate by and put in time in a traditional work environment."

Cali and Jody are now national advocates for their system—they are working with another Fortune 150 retailer and a Fortune 100 technology company that are in the process of becoming ROWEs, and a host of smaller companies have already made the transition.

But how can a ROWE possibly work in this economy? Best Buy, like so many retailers, has been struggling with sales, so will this freedom evaporate? On the contrary. Cali and Jody say because the system has actually increased productivity and often lowered fixed costs like real estate, it's actually expanding. "There is a huge competitive advantage baked in to ROWE in tough economic times because when leadership expects teams to 'tighten their belt,' everyone is able to voice whether activities are adding value or whether they're wasting time. Nobody wants wasted capacity in good times, but in tough times there is NO room for waste," Cali told us. "ROWE employees know how to get results and are relentlessly focused on that."

Deloitte and Touche

Anne Weisberg and Cathleen Benko of Deloitte and Touche were heavily focused on how to hang on to their valuable female workforce as the nation heads into a talent shortage. Even in an economic downturn, the fundamentals of America's demographics still apply. Over the next few years, the country will need productive talent to revive and expand its economy but a deficit of well-qualified labor still looms. For Deloitte, with a huge female workforce, it's a real structural problem. Weisberg and Benko came up with Mass Career Customization, thanks to an epiphany they had one day that just seemed obvious: if products can now be customized en masse, why not careers?

Every employee at Deloitte, not just women, now continually adjusts key aspects of their career. You can work less, work from different places, shoulder more or less responsibility. Basically, you can choose when to "dial up" and when to "dial down," with the knowledge that dialing up will get you promoted faster, and dialing down will slow promotions. Benko says what is so critical about the program is the attempt to *standardize* the idea of a flexible workplace. It removes the individual deal-making for flexible working conditions, which Benko said was creating confusion at Deloitte.

"We found that many people didn't like the old system," she says. "People would often say 'I just feel guilty or I feel like I'm letting my team down.' And we were also hearing, 'Am I eligible for the next level? Can I still get promoted?'"

Wal-Mart

Tom Mars is a present-day Johnny Appleseed on the subject of flexibility. As executive vice president and chief administrative officer of a behemoth-like Wal-Mart, he can change minds by planting ideas around the country, and he can use company muscle to force the business world to pay attention. Much as Wal-Mart's become a major player on the issue of sustainability, it's set to engender substantial change on the issue of flexibility. "Just a few years ago I was pretty dismissive of the idea of flextime," he admits ruefully. "I'm embarrassed at how shallow my thinking was. I think my attitudes were fairly typical of a lot of people. When anybody would raise it with me, I would think privately, 'We're trying to run a law department here.'"

But when he has an epiphany, Mars moves fast. A few years ago, when he was general counsel, he looked around at his almost all-white, all-male legal team after attending a legal diversity conference and decided to shake things up. Within a few years, the Wal-Mart legal department employed more than 40 percent women and more than 35 percent lawyers of color. That's a move he feels has so benefited the quality of the company's legal work that he's consistently used the $250 million worth of annual legal business the company does with other law firms to demand change. Wal-Mart noticed almost all of the relationship partners on their top 100 accounts were white men—so Mars asked for more women and minorities. Wal-Mart ended up moving $60 million in annual revenue to new women and minority relationship partners, converting their white male counterparts into the new minority group. And when Mars wasn't satisfied that several of Wal-Mart's outside law firms were embracing diversity, he dropped their business.

"You can understand that's just not the attitude we like in people representing our company around the country," Mars explains, in a folksy aw-shucks style that must have made his willingness to use the company's big stick something of a shock to these unenlightened firms.

As he was being feted for those achievements, Mars started reading information about why women have such a hard time making it through the ranks at law firms and companies. It was a lack of flexibility.

"I thought a lot about this, and frankly, I just decided to do it. I came in to the next staff meeting and told my team we needed to do it quickly and without bureaucracy, and to come up with a good policy within thirty days." He grins.

Today the legal team at the company works without any time boundaries.

"With the exception of a handful of bona fide workaholics, everybody takes advantage of the program. Everybody leaves during the week to go to soccer games and the like. Somebody reported to me recently they went to go see a movie," Mars says happily. "Our office has had a policy that office hours begin at seven-thirty, but nobody pays attention now. I run into a lawyer who comes into the building at 10 A.M., and frankly, the cool thing about it is I don't know if they're coming into work or if they've already been here and are coming back again. We just don't think about it anymore."

Wal-Mart also gives the 160 lawyers in the department the ability to cut back hours, or work from home a number of days week. Is he worried about clients or image or anything like that if an employee is with her children from three to seven, and then starts work again in the evening?

"In emergencies we're all flexible. But that's not common. These days I always tell people," he says with a shrug, "we're running a law department, not a fire department.

"There's no doubt in my mind that no matter how you measure morale, it's considerably higher than it ever was before," Mars concludes. "The element of trust that was introduced when we installed flextime has made not only happier people but better lawyers. They have a greater willingness to do their jobs, and to do them with appropriate independence."

Treat employees like grown-ups and we act like grown-ups. It's revolutionary.

By the way, Tom's innovation in Wal-Mart's legal department has caught the eye of other departments across the company, and many are moving to implement the changes wholesale. We love to emphasize the power of one, your power to affect change as an individual woman. Think of this as the power of one as well—one man who made big waves with his goliath of a company. Bravo.

Sun Microsystems

Sun Microsystems is the epitome of a company without walls, boundaries, or mandatory cubicles. There are employees around the world—from Beijing to Boston to Buenos Aires—working wherever they please. The issue of where an employee might live barely comes up in job interviews. Live where you want. Just get the job done.

Greg Papadopoulos, the chief technology officer for Sun Microsystems, laughs when we suggest that all California companies surely operate that way. Not so. There are plenty of California cultures with the attitude that "if I don't see your butt in the seat, or don't see you staying late, then you are not working hard enough," he says.

Papadopoulos says Sun embraced its Open Work Plan almost by accident, for practical reasons. They were growing so fast in the middle of the dot-com boom most managers realized it was literally impossible to fit everyone into their office space.

These days the plan is critical to company culture. Sun's Barbara Williams, a senior manager at the company says, with a perpetual smile on her face, that she works harder than ever because of her freedom. "People are just passionate about the workplace and the teams and what they do," she says, sparkling. "It's what drew me to Sun—the flexibility—and the amazing opportunity to thrive. So what if my boss is there at 10.30 A.M. I don't feel I need to be. If I'm more creative at 9 P.M. at night—great!"

The program was revolutionary for the company, critical not only in terms of cost-saving, but also in terms of productivity and talent retention. "It's all about gathering talent," says Papadopolous. "Technology creation is an art form."

Even today, as Sun tries to weather the economic challenges, it believes its Open Work Place Program is essential. "Our Open Work plan helps to define the company," says Ann Bamesberger, vice president of Sun's Open Work program. "More than that, it ensures that our fixed costs, like real estate, for example, remain reasonable, and that productivity stays high. It's exactly the sort of program that helps in a challenging economy."

The Right Stuff

OK. All that sounds great, you're probably thinking: But what are the odds I'm going to find a company like that? It's true that most companies don't have those breathtaking, eye-popping programs and stats to show off, at least not yet. Not every company is ready to, or is even able to, blow open its walls and structures and rules and set its stunned employees free. But you can still find smart companies and their managers who are tuned in to female work-life trends, and who are prepared to adapt to make things work, even within a more traditional structure.

Marriott

At the Marriott Company, which has an enormous female workforce, senior managers are well versed in what's coming—and that's a critical attitude to look for. "I do think the workplace is changing—I'm not even sure companies are aware that it's changing right underneath them," says David Rodriguez, executive vice president of HR at Marriott. "I fully expect that within the next five years this building will look quite different," he says, referring to Marriott headquarters in Maryland. "There will probably be more offices rented as needed and a lot of conference space facilities, teleconferencing. . . . I think it will be very different."

The company has the standard flextime, compressed work-week, and telecommuting policies on offer, but do the real star managers take advantage of these programs? Not so much, yet. A group of top women we had lunch with, when pressed, said they'd love to work, say, four days a week but didn't think a move like that would go over well. They still worry about perceptions. But Rodriguez tries to encourage his own team to work at least one day a week from home. He says they are more productive that way. And he's experimenting. He has a group of "flex-staffers" working on projects—managers who've worked at the company before and who are valued—but don't want to work full time. It may be that those women we had lunch with have more power than they think.

One example of the company's modern outlook is Laura Bates, a senior executive star, who recently resigned her post at Marriott to spend more time with her children. When she announced her decision, the company surprised her by offering interesting and well-paid contract work that would keep her connected. David Rodriguez hopes that when her children are older, Laura will choose to dial her career back up, at Marriott. "Somewhere, say three to five years out, we fully expect Laura is going to be part of our senior management somewhere in the company," he says confidently. "It's crucial to keep her connected."

PepsiCo

You might imagine the massive PepsiCo to be rigidly set in its corporate ways. Hardly. Even though they don't have a formal, all-inclusive flexibility program like Sun, for example, their management style is progressive. Working from home some of the time? Usually not a big deal, says Cynthia Trudell, the head of personnel and a senior vice president.

"Years ago there was a general attitude—'Oh my, if people

are working from home, they won't be working.'" She smiles. "But we believe, and this is literally around the globe, that if people don't have to be here and they can work from home, then they are in better control of their time."

It's a good sign when a company understands work can happen anywhere. It's even better when bosses *push* employees to create a less rigid existence. Let them know it's OK. PepsiCo cemented a program into its performance reviews called "One Simple Thing." It forces employees to name something not really work-related they'd like to accomplish—to do differently—that might change their routine at the office. Something they may be reluctant to do otherwise—like getting out early to the gym one day a week or working from home one morning.

And a critical thing to look for: can valued managers dial back for a while? Go part time? That is evaluated on a case-by-case basis, but productive employees get a yes whenever possible. Remember Angelique Krembs? She spent almost two years working from home part time. "Where it makes sense we will go out of our way," Trudell says. "When you work hard at bringing people in, making them part of the organization—if you need those skill sets in the long run it makes sense. It can be a win-win for everyone."

Even if the practice isn't yet thoroughly ingrained in company culture, or spelled out in a policy book, if you uncover at a prospective company open minds like they have at PepsiCo or Marriott, then the job you're looking at is a good bet. You have a chance to be a pioneer and poster child for the company, which is valuable for everyone.

Dot O'Brien

Or you might just get lucky enough to come upon an individual boss like Dot O'Brien. For the two lawyers she employs flexibly—i.e., for the hours they want to work and not more—Dorothy O'Brien gives this grade report: "I judge by results and how they're delivered, the skill with which they're delivered, and I believe these two lawyers deliver results that are certainly, at a minimum, equal to colleagues that may have to be here, or choose to be here for longer hours."

If you hear a sentiment like that, take the job. You will be in very good hands. Thank you, Dorothy, for recognizing what we know to be true.

What can we say—we're biased. We believe the most meaningful breakthroughs will come when companies stop treating flexible schedules as favors. Gazing out at nirvana, we think that when women, or men, have to give a reason for their "different" schedules, and this in turn means that bosses are then put in the position of having to judge whether or not those reasons are valid, then it results in an inherently unhealthy situation for the feng shui of a modern workplace. It makes some women, or men, nervous, so they don't ask, and it makes bosses even more nervous, so they don't offer. A spiral of resentment can build fast on both sides. We've spoken to many employers who find the situation incredibly awkward. "We don't want to choose between a one-year-old daughter, a sick parent, and an unfinished novel," they tell us. Most bosses simply don't want the responsibility of passing moral judgment on an employee's reasons for wanting to change their schedule.

We sympathize. Honestly. Who are we to say that one demand is "better" or more "valid" than another. We certainly don't care whether your desire to change your life is your children, as ours is, or your dog, or your lotus position.

But the solution to all of these employer concerns is beautifully simple, if you'll allow us to indulge in a little Womenomics advice to the CEO. Simply stop judging. Does it really matter if it's little Pat the toddler or big Pat the poodle that's driving the demand for change? So long, of course, as the work is getting done, the goals are being met, and the employee is producing as she should, why she leaves at 3 P.M., arrives at 10 A.M., or works from her spare room is really irrelevant.

In other words, it's the results, stupid.

"When you think of all of the ways it could go wrong, you won't change," warns Greg Papadopoulos of Sun. "It takes courage from the management side."

So woman up, corporate America! Are there concerns? Yes. Will it require some work? Yes.

But this is going to be a more pressing issue than ever in a flagging economy. All of the big business thinkers say the focus will *necessarily* shift to efficiency and productivity. The core tenants of Womenomics.

A more porous, more flexible, and more dynamic workplace is the business future, whether you see that now or not. "The shift is clearly toward that environment," agrees Bruce Tulgan. "It will happen underneath companies," agrees David Rodriguez, "and one day they will sort of say maybe we should ride this wave and let policies facilitate what's already happening."

The companies who understand the organic, all-encompassing nature of this tidal wave and embrace it are those who stand the best chance of beating the competition on every level. They will be first to the next frontier.

"At Wal-Mart we started experimenting with sustainability a few years ago, and nobody was thinking about it as a way to make our business more efficient or profitable," notes Tom Mars. "It was all about image and doing good. As we got in to it it's turned out to be unexpectedly helpful to the business, beyond anybody's wildest imagination. And I think, as we enter into this flextime and this workforce awareness paradigm, there's a clear parallel. It seems like the right thing to do, but soon everyone will see that the business case is just obvious."

How lucky, really, that we live in an era when letting people work the way they want to turns out to be good business, and good business in *any* economic climate. Sun can attract talent from all over the world. Capitol One can spin its positive energy into profits. And companies like PepsiCo and Marriott have the wisdom to understand how much they've invested in executives like Angelique Krembs and Laura Bates, and therefore they've said yes to their desire to work in a different way. They are looking beyond temporary career lulls and betting on the future with these women.

Like most things, it just boils down to simple economics. Or should we say, happily for us, Womenomics.

Take Womenomics with You

As you head off into work-life bliss, we want to give you a final bit of news you can *literally* use—at any moment. Here's a *Womenomics* cheat sheet you can cut out and keep in your wallet and pull out whenever you need to remind yourself how you *can* finally get what you want. If you want to stop all the juggling and struggling and finally live and work the way you really want to right now, here are five Womenomics facts you cannot do without:

ultimate news you can use

We've got the power. Companies want us and can't afford to lose us.

We're not alone. Four out of five of us want more flexibility at work.

Know what you really want from life and you can write your own rules for success.

Work smarter not harder and ask for what you want.

Flexibility is NOT a favor. Major corporations are embracing it—because it makes business sense in *any* economy.

epilogue

KATTY I still remember the morning Claire left an outraged message on my cell phone: "Are you crazy? I just heard you're seriously thinking of taking that White House reporting job! You know it'll make you miserable. You'll work round the clock and never see the kids. Listen, I've got a much better idea for us—let's write a book about how to work and have time." Even amid the crackles of the Verizon connection her enthusiasm and confidence were infectious.

CLAIRE "Come on, it'll be much better than getting into the White House at five every morning," I said jokingly. But in the course of that one conversation we found we were both serious and passionate. More passionate about this issue than any other. "We should tell some of the stories of how we've worked—and found time for our lives by saying no to those workaholic jobs. We always think our choices are crazy, but maybe we've got it right!"

When we began this book we thought we were telling our story. We soon discovered we were telling yours. This book is essentially the proposition that professional women can finally live and work the way we've always really wanted, though most of us have never dared to ask. We hope we've lifted the veil of secrecy and anxiety that often clouds this intensely sensitive issue.

The workplace is changing dramatically. It's struggling to meet a talent shortage, rushing to embrace the benefits of new technology, and working to modernize itself in ways that happen to call for a more "feminine" management style. We have more clout than ever before. The result will be that our desire for a saner work life will soon be embedded in all work practices. But until that happens, this is the guide to doing it for yourself. With Womenomics, you can reach a career-life balance that really does work for you, your family, your boss, and your future.

There's no question it's a revolution whose time has come. Innovation and change are flowing across governments, industries, and income levels.

- Wal-Mart is putting together a major report on the benefits of diversity and flexibility. As it did with sustainability, the company hopes to be a leader on the issue and then use its clout to push change across the marketplace.

- From the city of Houston to the state of Virginia, local governments are desperate to cut down on traffic and pollution. They're creating huge incentives for businesses to offer flextime.

- The recession is only hastening the trend. Companies that have already embraced flexibility see it as a tool to stay afloat in the crisis; from increased productivity to high morale, they say they can't survive without it. Other firms are starting to use furloughs, flexibility, and shortened workweeks as short-term methods to avoid layoffs. Once businesses see the productivity benefits, they won't go back. Through the lens of the crisis, female management skills—more inclusive, heavily focused on the long term, and less prone to risk taking—suddenly appear all the more valuable.

- First Lady Michelle Obama wants to make this her signature issue. She hopes to focus on creating support networks for the women who have no options—just the angst. "I've run into so many mothers," she told us, "who are working because they have to work and then they find their kids are in day care from seven in the morning until six at night. They have no choice, but they feel guilty."

Many of us are lucky. As professional women we often *do* have choices, even if they don't seem easy or obvious. It helps to remember that fact on days when the juggle seems too much. We have options less fortunate women can only dream of. Indeed we have more options than ever, because Womenomics is not about making the best of a bad deal; it's about building a better, happier, more productive future; a win-win all around.

It is true that right now most of the great work lives we've uncovered are being won by stressed-out individuals. They are women, perhaps just like you, who were on the verge of quitting, and figured there was nothing to lose in attempting one last conversation with their boss to ask for a more manageable deal. They are women who have gone down on bended knee and carved out more time on the hush-hush, often sworn to secrecy by nervous employers. But they get their bit of nirvana.

For many, but certainly not for all women, the demands of young children have pushed them to have that frightening, and once unimaginable, "I need to work from home/three days a week/fewer hours/more flexibly/two hundred days a year" conversation. That maternal instinct is a huge drive behind the demand for change, but it's not the only one. We've met plenty of other women (and men) who say they've changed schedules, scaled down, or switched things around just because they want a more manageable life—no kids, no sick mom, no triathlon, no reason other than just because. Just because, let's be honest, life is short, and who doesn't want more fulfillment.

As we said at the start of the book, you need this change, the corporate world needs this change, and the economy needs this change. And it may well be the moment, as the worldwide obsession with stratospheric wealth necessarily fades, that everyone finally gets it. Womenomics is about getting the values right for all of us.

But look, important change comes when this workplace sanity is no longer the result of agonized evenings, tearful Monday mornings, and screw-your-courage-to-the-sticking-post conversations in the corner office. It comes when there is institutional change. It comes when bosses realize en masse what we laid out right at the beginning of this book—that women mean good business and are worth keeping, and that happy employees are more productive. The paradigm shift comes when accommodating the demands of a woman's schedule is the norm rather than a favor. No questions asked, no judgments made, and no reasons given.

That's the moment when educated, valuable women will no longer leave their professional lives in droves, as they've been doing in recent years. That's the moment when companies will benefit from their huge talents and when the economy as a whole will be stronger for it.

When bosses start to measure employees on how they do their work rather than on where they do their work, then all the reasons for not allowing so-and-so to work such-and-such a schedule simply disappear. If an employee is achieving their targets, who cares when or where they work?

Companies like Capitol One, Best Buy, Sun Microsystems, Deloitte and Touche, Wal-Mart—they and many others really get it. They don't need to judge one reason over another, or worry about dominoes, or hand out flexible schedules like prizes at a children's birthday party. They simply ask their employees to do their jobs. They treat employees like grown-ups. And maybe, in the end, that is what all working women really aspire to—being given control and being treated like adults. It's simple, really.

That's the tipping point—the shift from favor to business strategy, from individual deal to institutionalized policy—which creates a *truly* flexible workplace.

Are we there yet? No. Are we well on the way? Most definitely.

It's only in the last thirty years that women have joined the professional world in any numbers. It is not surprising that our relationship with work is still evolving. What we have learned is that the model of the last three decades has not worked for us as it should.

But here's another Womenomics twist. Part of the original feminist argument was that the work world would never change until women got to the top and forced change upon it. That no longer holds. The corporate world is changing, not because of a female dictatorship, but because of our *collective* power as consumers and as valuable, but dissatisfied, workers.

Womenomics is a revolution ignited by two sparks. The first is that companies are realizing the increased productivity and profit that women generate, especially when they can work in the way that best suits them. The second comes from *you*, from women who are demanding change. In order to keep fueling the movement we need to keep pushing.

Our part of the revolution really does start inside each and every one of us with the question: What do I really want from life? Answer that honestly and confidently and you are ready to join the brigades who are saying "no" to business as usual.

We know it's hard when you feel like you are the only one. The only one struggling to do it all. The only one wondering why you feel so dissatisfied, even though you have gorgeous kids and a terrific career. The only one questioning whether you've simply lost your drive and ambition. The only one summoning up your courage to have "that conversation" with your boss. The only one wondering whether it means you just "don't have what it takes." But believe us you are not the only one. Far from it. All across the world millions of professional women face exactly the same dilemma as you do every single day. If there's one thing you must take away from Womenomics, it's that you are not alone.

Think of Womenomics as a modern-day manifesto, a working woman's call to arms. We hope you now believe you have the power to wage and win your battle. And while it's true that this individual fight for a precious little bit of flextime is far from ideal, remember, it is an evolutionary step. Take heart. One day, we believe, in the not too distant future, the advice in this book will be redundant because the idea of freedom at work will be commonplace. In our ideal world all careers in all companies will be so customized, altered, flexed, feminized, and, yes, balanced, that women will look back at this era and wonder what all the fuss was about.

Every employer we've interviewed sees this as the next big business trend. Few are brave enough to put a specific time frame on it as a universal proposition, but most think that within a decade the world of work will be unrecognizable.

Women and Womenomics will transform the workplace. Not long ago we were happy just to be at the boardroom table. Now we are refashioning, retooling, and rebuilding that table to suit our unique female tastes. We won't sit meekly anymore. If we meet resistance in one company, then we now know we are so valuable that another will welcome us with open, flexible arms.

There has never been a better time to be a professional woman. We have more power than ever to aim for the top, the middle, or anyplace we want.

Erin glances down at her watch. She's got a conference call in two hours. She e-mails a quick message to her assistant, Emily, who works from home today, to round up the troops. Bob will be on his cell, she remembers, checking out his son's new apartment. Denise is probably at the office by now, but her schedule tends to vary, depending on her husband's travel commitments. Sandy is in Turkey for a client meeting. For a moment she thinks back to her old, clock-watching boss and shakes her head. Her new team is superb, and everyone confirmed this morning that they'd read her notes and were ready to brainstorm on how to get the Wagner account.

This will be her first formal pitch as executive vice president! Erin feels that familiar rush—the thrill of going after new business coursing through her veins. She spent the morning running over creative concepts in her mind—and also running along the canal near her home. She smiles, drops her BlackBerry into her purse, and smoothes her skirt. She checks her watch again: 11 A.M. Right on time, Erin thinks happily, as she heads into her daughter's school for lunch duty.

endnotes

1. Matt Richtel. "More Companies Are Cutting Labor Costs Without Layoffs," *The New York Times*, December 22, 2008. Retrieved from http://www.nytimes.com/2008/12/22/business/22layoffs.html.

2. Michel Ferrary. "Why Women Managers Shine in a Downturn," *Financial Times*, March 2, 2009. Retrieved from http://www.ft.com/cms/s/0/40bb00ac–06cb–11de-ab0f–000077b07658.html?nclick_check=1.

3. "The Business Case for Gender Equality," *Women to the Top*. Retrieved from: http://www.women2top.net/uk/thatswhy.htm#whytop.

4. Roy Adler. "Women in the Executive Suite Correlates to High Profits." *European Project on Equal Pay*. Retrieved from: http://www.equalpay.nu/docs/en/adler_web.pdf.

5. Nicole Woolsey Biggert et al. "UC Davis Study of California Women Business Leaders," *UC David Graduate School of Management*, 2005. Retrieved from http://www.gsm.ucdavis.edu/uploadedFiles/Centers_of_Excellence/Center_for_Women_and_Leadership/2005UCDavisCAWomenBusLeadersStudy.pdf.

6. "The Bottom Line: Connecting Corporate Performance and Gender Diversity," *Catalyst*, January 2004.

7. "Postsecondary Institutions in the United States: Fall 2000," *U.S. Department of Education, National Center for Education Statistics*.

8. Elaine Chao. "Executive Women in Government," *Speeches by Secretary Elaine L. Chao, U.S. Department of Labor,* March 22, 2006. Retrieved from http://www.dol.gov/_sec/media/speeches/20060322_exec.htm.

9. "The Bottom Line: Connecting Corporate Performance and Gender Diversity," *Catalyst,* January 2004.

10. Yvonne Roberts. "You're Fired!" *The Guardian,* March 6, 2008.

11. "The 2003 Female FTSE Index," *Cranfield School of Management, Centre for Developing Women Business Leaders,* 2003.

12. Bob Sutton. "The War for Talent Is Back," *Harvard Business Publishing,* April 23, 2007.

13. Ibid.

14. "Management Futures: The World in 2018," *Chartered Management Institute,* March 2008.

15. "The Bottom Line: Connecting Corporate Performance and Gender Diversity," *Catalyst,* January 2004.

16. "Cars.com Adds Women Car Site to Network," *Consumer Lab Blog,* June 5, 2007.

17. "The Business Case for Gender Equality," *Women to the Top.* Retrieved from http://www.women2top.net/uk/thatswhy.htm#whytop.

18. Emmett C. Murphy. Talent IQ (LaCrosse: Platinum Press, 2007), Appendix B.

19. Charles Fishman. "The War for Talent," *Fast Company,* Issue 16, July 1998.

20. Mitra Toosi. "Labor Force Projections to 2016: More Workers in Their Golden Years," *Monthly Labor Review,* November 2007.

21. "Engaging and Retaining Talent," *The Human Capital Institute.* Retrieved from http://www.humancapitalinstitute.org/hci/tracks_engaging_retaining_talent.guid.

22. "Plateauing: Redefining Success at Work," Knowledge@Emory, November 8, 2006.

23. Jo Ind. "Flexible Working the Key to Business Success," *Birmingham Post*, October 27, 2008.

24. Simone De Beauvoir. *The Second Sex*, New York: Knopf, 1949, 53.

25. Rosie Boycott. "Why Women Don't Want Top Jobs, by a Feminist," *Daily Mail*, April 22, 2008.

26. Martha Lagace. "Getting Back on Course," Harvard Business School, September 4, 2001.

27. "Generation and Gender in the Workplace," Family and Work Institute, 2004.

28. Judy Pahren. Personal Interview.

29. Robin Ehlers. Personal Interview.

30. "The Business Case for Gender Equality," *Women to the Top*. Retrieved from: http://www.women2top.net/uk/thatswhy. htm#whytop.

31. "Generation and Gender in the Workplace," Family and Work Institute, 2004, and "The 2008 National Study of the Changing Work Force," Family and Work Institute.

32. "Women-Owned Businesses Grew at Twice the National Average," Census Bureau Report, January 26, 2006.

33. "The 2008 National Study of the Changing Work Force," Family and Work Institute.

34. Ibid.

35. Cathleen Benko. *Mass Career Customization*, Boston: Harvard Business School Press, 2007, 53.

36. "The 2008 National Study of the Changing Work Force," Family and Work Institute.

37. Ibid.

38. Ibid.

39. Ibid.

40. Elaine Chao. "Remarks Prepared for Delivery: National Summit on Retirement Savings, May 1, 2006," U.S. Department of Labor.

41. "Making Work 'Work': New Ideas from the Winners of the Alfred P. Sloan Awards for Business Excellence in Workplace Flexibility," Family and Work Institute, 2008.

42. Cathleen Benko. *Mass Career Customization*, Boston: Harvard Business School Press, 2007, 63.

43. "Why Women Are Wary," *Wall Street Journal*, September 21, 2005.

44. Cranfield University School of Management survey, "The Impact of Flexible Working Practices on Performance," April 30 2008.

45. http://arstechnica.com/news.ars/post/20070814-e-mail-stress-slowing-down-workers-say-researchers.html.

46. http://www.dailymail.co.uk/news/article–560166/Email-time-bandits-Office-staff-just-FOUR-hours-work-day-avalanche-messages.html.

47. http://edition.cnn.com/2005/WORLD/europe/04/22/text.iq/.